Helmut Meier

# Thomas Clarkson: 'Moral Steam Engine' or False Prophet?

## A Critical Approach to Three of his Antislavery Essays

Helmut Meier

# THOMAS CLARKSON: 'MORAL STEAM ENGINE' OR FALSE PROPHET?

## A Critical Approach to Three of his Antislavery Essays

*ibidem*-Verlag
Stuttgart

**Bibliografische Information der Deutschen Nationalbibliothek**
Die Deutsche Nationalbibliothek verzeichnet diese Publikation in der Deutschen Nationalbibliografie; detaillierte bibliografische Daten sind im Internet über http://dnb.d-nb.de abrufbar.

**Bibliographic information published by the Deutsche Nationalbibliothek**
Die Deutsche Nationalbibliothek lists this publication in the Deutsche Nationalbibliografie; detailed bibliographic data are available in the Internet at http://dnb.d-nb.de.

∞

Gedruckt auf alterungsbeständigem, säurefreien Papier
Printed on acid-free paper

ISBN-10: 3-89821-843-0

ISBN-13: 978-3-89821-843-6



Printed in Germany

Acknowledgements

I would like to thank Univ.-Prof. Mag. Dr. Wolfgang Zach, and Mag. Dr. Ulrich Pallua for their help with the present work, and of course my parents, who have always supported me during my studies both financially and in many other ways.

## 1 Introduction

Thomas Clarkson's significance for the British abolitionist movement was not only the immense personal effort he put into the abolition of the slave trade, but also that his many pamphlets and essays made him one of the chief ideologists of this unique movement. Although originally a divinity student, Clarkson won an essay competition on the topic of slavery at the University of Cambridge, after which he became increasingly involved in abolitionism, and a leading member of a number of British antislavery committees and societies. In the 1780s Clarkson famously travelled over 35,000 miles between the major British slave ports to collect evidence for presentation in Parliament.

Modern historical interpretations of the abolitionist movement are primarily concerned with questions about the validity of its moral claims. The abolitionists' self image and their depiction in earlier historical interpretations is one of moralist "Saints",[1] who were fighting for a cause against economic interests.[2] Starting with the work of Eric Williams this picture of abolitionism was increasingly questioned. Historians looked into the wider reasons for the movement's success, such as the social circumstances of the time.[3] Central to these interpretations is that they investigate the concurrence of the abolition of the slave trade and the development of modern, industrial, and urban British society, and the rise of a new, capitalist class.[4] Abolitionism is therefore often seen as part of the hegemonic process of the free-labour ideology. Thus the abolitionists' strategy of contrasting the British system of wage labour with colonial slavery, supported the first, and condemned the latter.[5] I will show in how far these elements can be found in Clarkson's work.

---

[1] Michael Jordan, *The Great Abolition Sham: The True Story of the End of the British Slave Trade* (Phoenix Mill, Thrupp, Stroud: Sutton Publishing, 2005) 85.

[2] cf. Seymour Drescher, *The Mighty Experiment: Free Labour versus Slavery in British Emancipation* (Oxford: University Press, 2002) 4.

[3] ibid.

[4] cf. Seymour Drescher, *Capitalism and Anti-slavery: British Mobilization in Comparative Perspective* (New York and Oxford: Oxford University Press, 1987) 162.

[5] cf. Thomas Bender, introduction, *The Anti-slavery Debate: Capitalism and Abolitionism as a Problem in Historical Interpretation* (Berkeley, Los Angeles and London: University of California Press, 1992) 4f.

The ideological affinity of capitalism and abolitionism, mentioned above, has far reaching consequences. Even the phenomenon of imperial colonialism is argued to have been underpinned and justified by the moralist claims of abolitionism: the abolition of the slave trade became part of the British rationale for their exertion of influence especially on the African continent.[6]

If these historical interpretations work, an interpretation of Thomas Clarkson's writings will fit in the conceptual framework they provide. Furthermore, an analysis should refer to, and be able to explain, later developments to a certain degree. In the present thesis I will try to make explicit the inherent ideology of Clarkson's essays, and to show in how far different interpretations are applicable. As a basis for this it is useful to link Clarkson's works to his life, which is why I will begin with some biographical notes about Thomas Clarkson, before turning to the analysis of his argumentative essays.

[6] cf. Drescher, *Capitalism and Anti-slavery* 165.

# 2 Thomas Clarkson's Biography

## 2.1 General Remarks

The main scholarly debate about British abolitionism is about its motivation, its origins, and its links to long-term historical developments. A main question of the debate seems to be whether abolishing the transatlantic slave trade was indeed the result of a wave of morality, just as it was initially seen, or if other reasons, like economic or political ones, were more important.[7]

In connection to that it is important to mention that most of Clarkson's biographers are influenced by the 'morality side' of the debate. Both Adam Hochschild in his *Bury the Chains,*[8] and Ellen Wilson in her biography,[9] use Samuel Taylor Coleridge's expression of the "moral steam engine"[10] when referring to Clarkson. I think that the narrative character of both works is probably the reason for these authors' tendency to make a hero out of their main 'character'.

In this thesis, however, I will try to use Clarkson's biography, and his description of the personal motives that led him to dedicate his life to the cause of abolishing the slave trade, as a starting point only for a critical analysis of his arguments and lines of thought.

Consequently, I will primarily deal with the earlier part of Clarkson's life and with how he describes his involvement with the abolitionist movement.

## 2.2 Early Life

Thomas Clarkson was born in Wisbech, Cambridgeshire in 1760. He was the son of a local schoolteacher. Clarkson was first educated at St. Paul's and then went up to St. John's College, Cambridge to study theology. He graduated from

---

[7] cf. Jordan, *The Great Abolition Sham* 85.

[8] Adam Hochschild, *Bury the Chains: The British Struggle to Abolish Slavery* (London: Pan Books, 2006) 85.

[9] Ellen Gibson Willson, *Thomas Clarkson: A Biography* (York: William Sessions Limited, 1989) 140.

[10] Hochschild, *Bury the Chains* 85.

Cambridge with honours in 1783. His involvement with the slave trade began when Peter Peckard, who was Cambridge's Vice-Chancellor at the time, chose the title "Anne Liceat Invitos in Servitutem Dare?"[11] for the annual competition for the best Latin dissertation. Clarkson partook in this competition and won it. In an often quoted passage of his *History of the Rise, Progress and Accomplishment of the Abolition of the African Slave Trade by the British Parliament*[12] (hereafter referred to as: Clarkson's *History)* he describes how he, "wholly ignorant of the subject",[13] primarily participated for academic honours first, but became increasingly emotionally agitated and involved while dealing with the subject of the slave trade in more depth:

> Furnished then in this manner, I began my work. But no person can tell the severe trial which the writing of it proved to me. I had expected pleasure from the invention of the arguments, from the arrangement of them, from the putting of them together, and from the thought in the interim that I was engaged in an innocent contest for literary honour. But, all my pleasure was damped by the facts which were now continually before me. It was but one gloomy subject from morning to night. In the day-time I was uneasy. In the night I had little rest. I sometimes never closed my eye-lids for grief. It became now not so much a trial for academical reputation, as for the production of a work, which might be useful to injured Africa. [...] I always slept with a candle in my room, that I might rise out of my bed and put down such thoughts as might occur to me in the night, if I judged them valuable, conceiving that no arguments of any moment should be lost in so great a cause. Having at length finished this painful task, I sent my Essay to the vice-chancellor, and soon afterwards found myself honoured as before with the first prize.[14]

Passages as the above are quite typical of Clarkson. They show his dramatic even slightly self important style.

## 2.3 "In Sight of Wades Mill"

After he had been awarded the first price for his Latin dissertation, he returned to London by horse. According to his own account in his *History* he kept on thinking about the issue of slavery during his trip. And it was in Hertfordshire,

---

[11] Translation: "Is it Right to Make Slaves of Others Against their Will?"

[12] Thomas Clarkson, *The History of the Rise, Progress and Accomplishment of the Abolition of the African Slave Trade by the British Parliament,* 1839 (Whitefish: Kessinger Publishing, no year); also available at: "The History of the Rise...," *Project Gutenberg* (7.Aug.2006 http://www.gutenberg.org/files/10633/10633-h/10633-h.htm).

[13] ibid. 117 (chap VII).

[14] Clarkson, *History* 118 (chap VII).

"in sight of Wades Mill"[15], that the pivotal moment in Clarkson's life occurred, none of Clarkson biographers fails to recount this:

> On returning to London, the subject [of his dissertation] almost wholly engrossed my thoughts. I became at times very seriously affected while upon the road. I stopped my horse occasionally, and dismounted and walked. I frequently tried to persuade myself in these intervals that the contents of my Essay could not be true. The more, however, I reflected upon them, or rather upon the authorities on which they were founded, the more I gave them credit. Coming in sight of Wades Mill, in Hertfordshire, I sat down disconsolate on the turf by the roadside and held my horse. Here a thought came into my mind, that if the contents of the Essay were true, it was time some person should see these calamities to their end. Agitated in this manner, I reached home. This was in the summer of 1785.[16]

The extract shows Clarkson's personal explanation for his later involvement with abolition, which was primarily a moral one; as I will point out later some of the arguments he uses in the extended translation of his Latin dissertation, *An Essay on the Slavery and Commerce of the Human Species, Particularly the African...*[17] (hereafter referred to as Clarkson's *Essay),* are also drawn from religious and moral considerations. I will, however, show in the subsequent chapters that there exists an incongruity between these motives and the arguments he uses in his later essays. Hochschild and Oldfield repeat Clarkson's heroic self-perception, relatively uncritically, in their respective works. Hochschild calls this moment "a landmark on the long, tortuous path to the modern conception of universal human rights"[18] and Oldfield[19] speaks of it as the moment of birth of Clarkson's involvement in the cause of abolition which finally led to its accomplishment. In 1979 a memorial stone was erected on the spot of Clarkson's spiritual experience, reading: "On this spot where stands this

---

[15] ibid.

[16] ibid.

[17] Thomas Clarkson, *An Essay on the Slavery and Commerce of the Human Species, Particularly the African, Translated form a Latin Dissertation, which was Honoured with the First Prize in the University of Cambridge, for the Year 1785, With Additions,* 1786 (Whitefish: Kessinger Publishing, no year); also available at: "An Essay on the Slavery...," *Project Gutenberg* (7.Aug.2006 http://www.gutenberg.org/files/10611/10611-h/10611-h.htm).

[18] Hochschild, *Bury the Chains* 89.

[19] John R. Oldfield, *Popular Politics and British Ant-Slavery: The Mobilisation of Public Opinion against the Slave Trade, 1787-1807* (London: Frank Cass Publishers, 1998) 71.

monument in the month of June 1785 Thomas Clarkson resolved to devote his life to bringing about the abolition of the slave trade."[20]

While it might not be justified to doubt the sincerity and integrity of Clarkson's motives, it is nevertheless important to place the impact of Clarkson's and the other abolitionists' arguments in a larger context and to try to take into account the overall historical developments of the time. Living at the time of the French and the Industrial Revolution, the abolitionists' actions and convictions were subject to the social and political changes of their time.

### 2.4 Meeting other Abolitionists

After this moment of epiphany Clarkson decided to translate his dissertation and to "enlarge it usefully"[21] so as to make it available to a wider audience. When he was in London looking for a publisher he met Joseph Hancock, who introduced him to the bookseller James Phillip. Phillip not only agreed to publish the *Essay*, but introduced Clarkson to several of the people who were later to found the 'London Committee for the Abolition of the Slave Trade.' The first of those was the Quaker William Dillwyn, whom he visited at his home on March 13, 1786:

> [...] William Dillwyn wished very much to see me at his house at Walthamstow, I appointed the 13th of March to spend the day with them there. We talked for the most part, during my stay, on the subject of my essay. [...] how surprised was I to hear, in the course of our conversation, of the labours of Granville Sharp, of the writings of Ramsay, [...] How surprised was I to learn that William Dillwyn himself had, two years before, associated himself with five others for the purpose of enlightening the public mind upon this great subject! How astonished was I to find that a society had been formed in America for the same object, with some of the principal members of which he was intimately acquainted! And how still more astonished at the inference which instantly rushed upon my mind, that he was capable of being made the great medium of connexion between them all.[22]

In his *History* Clarkson describes the origins of the antislavery movement as coming from four classes of forerunners. The first of these classes consists of "persons in Great Britain of various descriptions",[23] including James Ramsay, Granville Sharp, and notably Adam Smith. The second and third classes are the Quakers in England and America among them William Dillwyn and Anthony

---

[20] Simon Kershaw, *The Good & The Great: Thomas Clarkson.* (08.08.2006, http://ely.anglican.org/about/good_and_great/tclarkson.html)

[21] Clarkson, *History* 119 (chap VII).

[22] ibid. 120/121 (chap VII).

[23] ibid. 44 (chap III).

Benezet, respectively. The writings of the latter exerted great influence over Clarkson's *Essay*. Dillwyn is seen by Clarkson as "the great medium of connection"[24] between the different classes. The idea of the unrighteousness of slavery had first occurred in Quaker circles on both sides of the Atlantic. Although David Brion Davis calls the Quakers the vanguard of the industrial revolution,[25] their strict religious ideology was by no means mainstream in the 18th century.[26] In his later work Clarkson seems to have realized that and increasingly relied on other than religious arguments. The fourth class consists of Dr. Peckard, the Vice-Chancellor of Cambridge, and of Clarkson himself.

Probably influenced by Linnaean taxonomy he illustrated the connections and mutual influence between those different classes by means of a map in which the classes are displayed as rivers joining up in one cause. This taxonomical way of arranging fact in a hierarchy is a technique that will be found throughout Clarkson's work. It has been commented that this lends the meeting of the different individuals forming the first abolitionist committee an element of divine inevitability.[27] Consequently, Clarkson describes his acquaintance with Dillwyn as an act of God: "My mind was overwhelmed with the thought that I had been providentially directed to his house; that the finger of Providence was beginning to be discernible; that the day-star of African liberty was rising, and that probably I might be permitted to become an humble instrument in promoting it".[28]

---

[24] ibid. 111 (chap VI).

[25] cf. David Brion Davis, "The Problem of Slavery in the Age of Revolution, 1770-1823," *The Anti-slavery Debate: Capitalism and Abolitionism as a Problem in Historical Interpretation,* ed. Thomas Bender (Berkeley, Los Angeles and London: University of California Press, 1992) 45.

[26] cf. Hochschild, *Bury the Chains* 77f.

[27] cf. Howard Temperley, "Anti-Slavery as a Form of Cultural Imperialsm," *Anti-Slavery, Religion, and Reform: Essays in Memory of Roger Anstey,* eds. Christine Bolt and Seymour Drescher (Hamden: Dawson, 1980) 337.

[28] Clarkson, *History* 121 (chap VII).

## 2.5 Becoming a Full-Time Reformer

It was, however, only in 1786 that Clarkson spent a month at James Ramsey's house in Teston, Kent and decided to devote himself fully to the cause of abolition. After having pledged himself a bit hastily to take up abolitionism full-time one evening at dinner, he determined "to give the subject a full consideration, and accordingly [he] walked to the place of [his] usual meditations, - the woods."[29] Clarkson was conscious of the fact that "a little labour now and then" would not suffice to see the slave trade to an end and that whoever took up this matter had to "devote [himself] wholly to it".[30] Since he could see no person other than himself to do that, he pondered on the arguments for and against such a decision.

Among the arguments in favour of it he states that there was never any "cause, which had been taken up by man in any country or in any age, so great and important; that never was there one in which so much misery was heard to cry for redress; that never was there one in which so much good could be done;"[31] in short: that there was "never one more worthy of the devotion of a whole life towards it."[32] On the other hand he considered his possible career in the Church, and that his "prospects there on account of his connexions were [...] brilliant."[33] He states that the "sacrifice of [his] prospects staggered [him] [...] most" because he had a "thirst after worldly interest and honours" which he could not "extinguish at once".[34] In the end, as we know, he "yielded, not because [he] saw any reasonable prospect of success in [his] new undertaking (for all cool-headed and cool-hearted men would have pronounced against it), but in obedience [...] to a higher Power." [35] One can see that Clarkson wanted the public to see himself as reluctantly making a sacrifice because he had to obey divine inspiration.

---

[29] ibid. 125 (chap VIII).
[30] ibid.
[31] ibid. 126 (chap VIII).
[32] ibid.
[33] ibid.
[34] ibid.
[35] ibid.

In May 1787 Clarkson was one of the twelve men who formed the Society for the Abolition of the African Slave Trade and its London Committee. In his *History* Clarkson describes the meeting of the founding members of the Committee as inevitable and providential. As already mentioned, he shows how the four different classes of forerunners[36] came together by means of a map using the picture of coalescing rivers (i.e. the individuals and their connections) joining into one big stream (i.e. the abolition movement), to become "the torrent which swept away the Slave trade."[37] The different forerunners influenced each other "by a process of intellectual diffusion".[38] For Clarkson Christianity was the main connecting force between the individuals and thus the ultimate reason why the slave trade was abolished. This version, with its emphasis on Christianity and moral, has been subject to much critique. Eric Williams, for example, was the first to take a radically different stance, "presenting the issue largely in terms of the interplay of economic interests".[39]

## 2.6 "Two Distinct Evils"

In the eyes of the abolitionists two 'evils' were to be removed: "The evil of the slave trade"[40] and "the evil of slavery itself".[41] Consequently, on March 24th, 1787 the Committee met to discuss which of the two to tackle first. They decided to take up the abolition of the transatlantic slave trade because the "removal of both would be to aim at too much, and that by doing this [they] might lose all".[42] Furthermore, they reasoned that by really abolishing the trade, "the bad usage of the slaves in the colonies [...] if not slavery itself, would fall"[43] and that the slaves would, in consequence, be emancipated when they were "fit for it".[44] Clarkson describes it as "laying the axe at the very root"[45] of

---

[36] cf. ibid. 39ff (chaps. II-X)
[37] Temperley, *Anti-Slavery as Cultural Imperialism* 338.
[38] ibid.
[39] ibid.
[40] Clarkson, *History* 148 (chap XIII).
[41] ibid.
[42] ibid.
[43] ibid.
[44] ibid. 149.
[45] ibid.

the evil, without evoking the objection of meddling with the property of the planters. An other argument was that it would be easier for the British government to enforce and control the abolition of the trade, by "station[ing] its ships of war, and command[ing] its custom-houses" without having to interfere with internal affairs of the West Indian colonies.[46]

This decision is typical of Clarkson's and the other Abolitionists' strategy. I will later show that, also in his essays, Clarkson never develops anything that could be called 'revolutionary potential', he always very much argues within the framework of what was socially acceptable and achievable. Howard Temperly also suggests that it is "more plausible to suppose that the antislavery marched in step with, and not in opposition to, the major trends of the period."[47]

## 2.7 Later Life

With William Wilberforce the abolitionists had a member of Parliament in favour of their cause. Their next step was to find evidence of the cruel and inhuman character of the trade, which could be used in parliamentary inquiries.

In the following years Clarkson took on the role of a fact-finder for the Society and famously travelled 35,000 miles between the main slave ports of Great Britain in order to get information about the trade right from the "fountainhead"[48] and to support local abolitionist committees, which were founded to petition parliament and to support the Society.

Clarkson's Quaker friends supplied him with an excellent network of families in different cities across the country, whom he could call on. As Clarkson publicly opposed the slave trade, for example in discussions in public houses, his mission was at times quite dangerous. He was even physically attacked by supporters of the trade and relates a scene in Liverpool in which he was assailed by a group of sailors:

> The temper of many of the interested people of Liverpool had now become still more irritable, and their hostility more apparent than before. I received anonymous letters, entreating me to leave it, or I should otherwise never leave it alive. [...]I noticed eight or nine persons making towards me [...] I expected that they would have divided to let me through them; instead of which they closed upon me and bore

---

[46] ibid.

[47] Temperley, *Slavery as Cultural Imperialism* 342.

[48] Clarkson, *History* 186 (chap. XVII).

> me back. I was borne within a yard of the precipice, when I discovered my danger; and perceiving among them the murderer of Peter Green [...], it instantly struck me that they had a design to throw me over the pier-head; [...] There was not a moment to lose. Vigorous on account of the danger, I darted forward. One of them, against whom I pushed myself, fell down: their ranks were broken; and I escaped, not without blows, amidst their imprecations and abuse.[49]

Clarkson's main aim was to get hold of the slave ships' muster rolls, death lists, and statements by sailors and ships' surgeons on the conditions during their journeys to the coast of Africa, the West Indian sugar colonies and back. He used the gathered material not only to reveal the terrible conditions of the slaves during the middle passage (i.e. from the Coast of Africa to the Caribbean islands) but also the cruel treatment and high mortality rates of the crew during the whole journey. In his *Essay on the Impolicy of the African Slave Trade*[50] (hereafter referred to as Clarkson's *Impolicy)* he shows that the slave trade lost more seamen in one year than all the other branches of overseas trade in two.

The facts he supplied to the Society were used by William Wilberforce in parliamentary debates. Based on his findings Clarkson wrote several books, essays and pamphlets between 1787 and 1794. In autumn 1789 he even travelled to Paris in an unsuccessful attempt to persuade the new French government to abolish the trade.

Upon his return to England Clarkson continued to travel in search of evidence straining himself so much that he had to retire in 1794 out of exhaustion. However, it took the abolitionists until 1807 to manage to get a bill against the slave trade through British Parliament. In 1808 Clarkson, pressed by the members of the Society, wrote his *History.* Upon finally winning the struggle for the abolition of the slave trade, he remarks not without some self-praise:

> It [i.e.the struggle] has furnished us also with important lessons. It has proved what a creature man is! how devoted he is to his own interest! to what a length of atrocity he can go, unless fortified by religious principle! But as if this part of the prospect would be too afflicting, it has proved to us, on the other hand, what a glorious instrument he may become in the hands of his Maker; and that a little virtue, when properly leavened, is made capable of counteracting the effects of a mass of vice![51]

---

[49] ibid. 199 (chap XVIII).

[50] Thomas Clarkson, *An Essay on the Impolicy of the African Slave Trade,* 1788 (Freeport and New York: Books for Libraries Press, 1971) 50.

[51] Clarkson, *History* 500 (chap XXXIII).

I think it is not hard to guess who Clarkson thinks to be the "glorious instrument" in the quote. Although his role in the abolitionist movement is certainly not to be underestimated, some of the critique concerning his self-importance, as uttered for example by Wilberforce's sons in their biography of their father[52], might be justified.

It remains to be said that Clarkson was a leading member of each of the three early Antislavery Societies: the Committee for the Abolition of the Slave Trade (later, the Society for the Abolition of the Slave Trade), founded in 1787; the Society for the Mitigation and Gradual Abolition of Slavery throughout the British Dominions, founded in 1807; and the British and Foreign Antislavery Society, founded in 1839.[53]

In 1823 a campaign for the emancipation of the West Indian slaves was launched for which Clarkson wrote his *Thoughts on the Necessity of Improving the Condition of the Slaves in the British Colonies, With a View to their Ultimate Emancipation; and on the Practicability, the Safety, and the Advantages of the Latter Measure* (hereafter referred to as Clarkson's *Thoughts*). In 1833 the British Parliament finally passed a bill that made slavery illegal in all of the country's dominions. Thomas Clarkson lived to see this and died in 1846.

---

[52] cf. Oldfield 70. and Brycchan Carey, *Biography of Thomas Clarkson,* 2002 (08.08.2006 http://www.brycchancarey.com/abolition/clarkson.htm).

[53] cf. "Thomas Clarkson," *The Anti-slavery Society* (22.Aug. 2006 http://www.anti-slaverysociety.org/).

## 3 Methodology

Having now established some basic facts about his life and work the remaining part of my thesis will be concerned with analysing Clarkson's argumentative writings in more depth. I will attempt to do a critical discourse analysis of Thomas Clarkson's argumentative essays, as part of anti–slavery discourse. In his essay "Multidisciplinary CDA: a plea for diversity", Teun van Dijk describes critical discourse analysis as discourse analysis with an attitude. He suggests an analysis of a social issue as a first step.[54] Here, one could of course take the point of view of the antislavery-movement itself, in which case the social issues would be such phenomena as transatlantic slave trade, West Indian slavery, and also abolition as such. This, however, would probably not lead to a very profound analysis. A better approach to abolitionism is certainly to be critical of it, and its goals. Therefore the achievements of the antislavery movement must not be viewed uncritically. Starting points for critique can be that antislavery discourse idealizes wage labour, and shows early imperialist elements as well as racist tendencies. In order to arrive at a more subtle picture of the British antislavery movement, the next chapter will deal with the different historical interpretations of the British antislavery movement.

### 3.1 Historical Interpretations and Criticism

Up to WWII most historians adopted a very distinct view of the "British Struggle"[55] against Slavery. Britain's leading role in connection with abolition had led to a sort of "national triumphalism"[56] in historiography, standing in the tradition of Clarkson's *History*. Hochschild's *Bury the Chains* is still influenced by this, as the second part of the title "The British Struggle to Abolish Slavery" shows. Accordingly, the moral and heroic dimensions of the "struggle" held the centre stage. In their survey of the scholarly debate of British antislavery both

---

[54] cf. Teun A. Van Dijk, „Multidisciplinary CDA: A Plea for Diversity," *Methods of Critical Discourse Analysis,* eds. Ruth Wodak and Michael Meyer (London: Sage Publications 2001) 98.

[55] Hochschild, *Bury the Chains* iv.

[56] Seymour Drescher, *The Mighty Experiment* 4.

Seymour Drescher[57] and Thomas Bender[58] cite Eric Williams's *Capitalism and Slavery,* and his hypothesis that it was not the moral claims of the abolitionists but rather economic interest that brought slavery in the West Indies to an end, as a seminal work in the field. What Williams saw as the main reason for the success of the antislavery movement, was that the plantation economy in the Caribbean was a declining branch of economy. Although this is still not an established fact,[59] Williams was the first to question the connection between the rise of capitalism and the abolition of slavery. Williams's new interpretation and the resulting questions about social and economic determination of culture triggered a different form of debate, giving rise to Marxist, Feminist, Anti-colonialist and Social-Scientific perspectives in the scholarly investigation of abolition.

In his work *Slavery in the Age of Revolution,* David Brion Davis raises the issue of class interest. What he suggests is that in connection with the rise of the middle classes, the concern for slave labour abroad might well have served the hegemonic function of legitimating free labour, and the methods of procuring it at home. Seeing them as the "very embodiment of the capitalist mentality, the English Quakers were in the vanguard of the industrial revolution;"[60] accordingly, Davis describes abolitionism as a "highly selective response to labour exploitation"[61] which was "in the interest of a capitalist class concerned with labor discipline and the legitimation of novel economic practices."[62] He does not, however, interpret the economic determination of the abolitionists' motives in a simplistic way. That is, he does not cynically interpret them as manipulating the issue of abolition to their own advantage. The main question for Davis is "the relationship between antislavery and the social system as a

---

[57] cf. ibid.
[58] cf. Bender, *Introduction* 1f.
[59] cf. Seymour Drescher, *Econocide : British Slavery in the Era of Abolition* (Pittsburgh, Pa. : Univ. of Pittsburgh Press, 1977) 15.
[60] Davis, "Slavery in the Age of Revolution" 45.
[61] ibid. 61.
[62] Bender, *Introduction* 5.

whole"[63] and how antislavery reinforced or legitimised the hegemony of a developing capitalist elite.[64]

Bender describes Davis's idea in the following way: "the focus on one kind of human exploitation seems to have sustained a language of social concern that offered a less critical perspective on other forms of exploitation, particularly that of workers suffering through the transition to modern capitalism."[65] Yet Davis argues that "ideological hegemony is not the product of conscious choice and seldom involves insincerity or deliberate deception."[66]

The vague but flexible connection between the intentions of the abolitionists and the long term effects and consequences of their actions and ideas gave rise to Thomas Haskell's critique of Davis's theories.[67] To attribute unconscious intentions to a group is problematic for him. He argues that "even conscious intentions are notoriously difficult to nail down in the absence of explicit statements of purpose, and unconscious intentions are still more problematic. By definition, they leave no direct empirical trace."[68] In turn Haskell favours Max Weber's concept of "elective affinity".[69] Capitalism favoured maxims of prudence founded on foresight of consequences, Haskell argues.[70] Thus, a form of life emerged "that made attention of the remote consequences of one's acts (or omissions) an emblem of civilization itself;"[71] accordingly, people felt more

---

[63] Davis, "Slavery in the Age of Revolution" 70.
[64]cf. ibid. 71.
[65] Bender, *Introduction* 5.
[66] Davis, "Slavery in the Age of Revolution" 71.
[67] cf. Thomas L. Haskell, "Capitalism and the Origins of Humanitarian Sensiblity , Part 1," *The Anti-slavery Debate: Capitalism and Abolitionism as a Problem in Historical Interpretation,* ed. Thomas Bender (Berkeley, Los Angeles and London: University of California Press, 1992) 116.
[68] Haskell, "Capitalism and Sensibility: Part 1" 122.
[69] Bender, *Introduction* 6.
[70] cf. ibid. 7.
[71] Thomas L. Haskell, "Capitalism and the Origins of Humanitarian Sensiblity , Part 2" *The Anti-slavery Debate: Capitalism and Abolitionism as a Problem in Historical Interpretation,* ed. Thomas Bender (Berkeley, Los Angeles and London: University of California Press, 1992) 155.

obliged to go to the aid of a suffering stranger. The role of capitalism in freeing the slaves for Haskell is creating a "precondition, albeit a vital one."[72]

A different position is held by John Ashworth who argues that in the American South, although strongly involved in international trade, no such thing as a dominant antislavery movement emerged, therefore, he argues that class interest must have played a part in British abolitionism.[73] He reasons that a partial social experience can lead to a partial view. For him the rise of wage labour and the acknowledgement of the importance of self interest made the foundations of public and private morals unstable. Therefore, those who embraced the new economy were strongly in need of a theory for social morality which worked for a self-interested world. The abolitionists, he says, supplied this theory. For him the rhetoric of the abolitionists is a theory of capitalist morality depending on a set of family values and a notion of free agency, which is denied by slavery.[74]

Seymour Drescher considers the rise of the cultural status of science during the 18th century and the resulting intrusion of social sciences into the slavery debate to be an important aspect of British abolitionism. For him the progress from medieval servitude to modern, free labour is part of the classical enlightenment paradigm. Drescher regards three social sciences as being of foremost importance. Firstly, political economy was the most popular source of authority, which directly provoked and answered questions about the relative superiority of free versus slave labour. Secondly, demography raised questions about the reproductive performance of slaves and non-slaves and the role of population pressure in transition from slavery to freedom. And finally, racial and epidemiological science called attention to biological aspects of race-based slavery. Consequently he sees the classic works of Adam Smith, and Thomas Robert Malthus as being the most important sources of scientific authority for the discussion of slavery.[75]

---

[72] Haskell, "Capitalism and Sensibility: Part 2" 155.

[73] cf. John Ashworth, *Capitalism and Humanitarianism The Anti-slavery Debate: Capitalism and Abolitionism as a Problem in Historical Interpretation,* ed. Thomas Bender (Berkeley, Los Angeles and London: University of California Press, 1992) 187.

[74] cf. Bender, *Introduction* 9f.

[75] cf. Drescher, *The Mighty Experiment* 4-7.

## 3.2 Critical Discourse Analysis

What all these approaches so far have in common is that they are interested in the connection between the abolition of slavery and the emergence of a new social order determined by capitalism. Although some are primarily interested in the connection between abolitionism and its contemporary society in Britain, however, a consideration of the long-term effects which abolitionist ideology had on the British colonial world adds a global dimension. Drescher, for example, states that antislavery ideology was a justifier for British imperialism,[76] and also David points out that this ideology encouraged a more direct British colonial intervention in Africa.[77]

In this context the definition of the term 'ideology' is an important one. According to Althusser, ideology interpellates individuals as subjects by making them accept the ruling classes' explanations of (social-) reality. In a way, ideology tells the individual what to take for 'common sense.'[78] In my attempt at a critical reception of Clarkson's texts I will try to analyse the underpinning ideology by taking a look at what the author depicts as 'common sense', and also at his implicit assumptions.[79] Van Dijk refers to the persuasiveness of a discourse due to the "social opinions that that are 'hidden' in its implicit premises and thus taken for granted by the recipients."[80] Clarkson's arguments will have to be treated as ideological entities.

Therefore it makes little sense to blame the abolitionists for consciously deceiving their audiences in order to establish the unequal power relations of an emerging capitalist and imperialist social order. It is obvious that they just chose such arguments in their essays that appealed to their contemporary society. David Turley writes that, in order to be successful in their struggle, the

---

[76] cf. Drescher, *Capitalism and Anti-slavery* 165.

[77] cf. David Brion Davis, "Slavery and 'Progress,'" *Anti-Slavery, Religion, and Reform: Essays in Memory of Roger Anstey,* eds. Christine Bolt and Seymour Drescher (Folkestone, Kent: Dawson Archon, 1980) 363.

[78] cf. Chris Barker, *Cultural Studies: Theory and Practice,* 2nd. ed. (London, Thousand Oaks, New Delhi: Sage Publications, 2004) 77f.

[79] cf. Norman Fairclough, *Language and Power*, 2nd ed. (Harlow: Pearson Education Limited, 2001) 69f.

[80] Teun A. van Dijk, "Critical Discourse Analysis," *The Handbook of Discourse Analysis,* eds. Deborah Schiffrin, Deborah Tannen, and Heidi E. Hamilton (Oxford: Blackwell, 2001) 358.

abolitionists had to come to terms with a contemporary British culture that offered them only a limited number of forms and channels through which to effect change.[81] Therefore the reason for the success of the abolitionist movement might be found in a general acceptance of their basic assumptions by British society at large. Identifying such hegemonic thoughts can again offer insights into a society's ideology.[82] Gaining general acceptance is a historical process determined by cultural, economic, and social factors and interests. Norman Fairclough stresses that discourse as a whole is historical.[83] Thus it will also be of importance to analyse in how far Clarkson draws on historical traditions and examples to support his arguments and also to try to show the hidden sources and the history of his ideas.

In his *Language and Power* Fairclough emphasises the importance of power relations as discursive elements. In his approach to critical language study he suggests an analysis of the way in which "language contributes to the domination of some people by others."[84] His approach, too, emphasises "'common-sense' assumptions which are implicit in the conventions according to which people interact."[85] These assumptions are the ideologies that reproduce unequal power relations.[86] In order to investigate the relationship between abolitionist texts and society at large, specific ideological elements within Clarkson's arguments will have to be analysed. In connection with slavery, unequal power relations do not only exist 'within' British society but on a global level as well. Therefore scholars suggest a connection between abolition and imperialism. Howard Temperley, for example, sees antislavery as a sort of cultural imperialism working in a "process of cultural triangulation whereby individuals and societies locate themselves in relation to history and to the world

[81] cf. David Turley, *The Culture of English Anti-slavery: 1780-1860* (London: Routledge, 1991) 3.

[82] cf. Antonio Gramsci, *Selections from the Prison Notebook*, eds. Quintin Hoare and Geoffrey Nowell Smith (New York: International Publishers, 1971) 325.

[83] cf. van Dijk, *Critical Discourse Analysis* 353.

[84] Fairclough, *Language and Power* 1.

[85] ibid. 2.

[86] cf. ibid. 2.

about them."[87] It will be important to identify such abolitionist ideology which might have influenced imperialism and also to analyse the image of Africa conveyed in Clarkson's work. As I have already mentioned, also Seymour Drescher writes that abolitionism worked as a legitimizer for European expansion,[88] and Davis proposes that "antislavery helped to justify the subjection of entire peoples to colonial rule, supposedly for the good of their future civilization."[89]

Antislavery ideology, therefore, can be seen as part of the post-slavery imperialist systems of colonial administration. Even Adam Hochschild states that the abolitionists did not set out to remove the social injustice of the colonial system but rather to make better servants to their masters out of the freed slaves.[90] Investigating the colonial and imperialist dimensions of abolitionism and the resulting unequal power relations provides the social issue which van Dijk suggests that critical discourse analysis should be concerned with.[91] I will, therefore, try to investigate which of the abolitionists ideas resonated with the British colonial system.

For a thorough ideological analysis of Clarkson's work, certain discursive parameters have to be defined in order to be able to categorize arguments. It makes sense to introduce these parameters according to their ideological source. Important sources for antislavery discourse are (in alphabetic order):

- Economy
- History
- Humanitarianism
- National Ideas
- Natural Law
- Racial Ideas
- Religion
- Specific(e.g. British-) Law

---

[87] Temperley, *Anti-Slavery as Cultural Imperialism* 333.
[88] cf. Drescher, *Capitalism and Anti-slavery* 165.
[89] Davis, *Slavery and 'Progress'* 363.
[90] cf. Hochschild, *Bury the Chains* 324.
[91] cf. van Dijk, *Critical Discourse Analysis* 352.

I think the most clear cut parameter is the term economy, under which I will sum up all of Clarkson's arguments that point to the monetary consequences of abolition, be that advantages or disadvantages. 'History' will obviously deal with the way the author constructs the past and uses it for the sake of his arguments.

Others, however, are more difficult to deal with. 'National-' and 'racial ideas' mutually influence each other. The OED defines 'national' as "having to do with nation,"[92] and 'nation' as "a large group of people sharing the same culture, language and history, and inhabiting a particular state or area."[93] The concept of 'race' on the other hand is defined as "1. each of the major divisions of humankind, based on particular physical characteristics. 2. racial origin and qualities associated with this […] 3. a group of people sharing the same culture, language etc. […]"[94] From these definitions it follows that the two concepts certainly overlap and mutually influence each other. Probably even more so in the late 18th and early 19th century when a concept of nation increasingly based on race started to emerge.[95] Therefore, the racial parameter of my analysis will be concerned with physical markers such as the Africans' blackness, whereas the national parameter will refer to ideas that deal with the interests or the character of a whole people. In connection with both of them the use of stereotypes will have to be investigated.

The difference between 'specific law' and 'natural law' can be established by looking at the respective sources. Arguments based on the specific laws of a certain state are referred to as 'specific law.' The 'natural law' parameter on the other hand, comprises arguments standing in the tradition of the philosophers John Locke and Thomas Hobbes. To explain this concept further it can be said that Clarkson adheres to Hobbes' definition of nature as "the art whereby God hath made and governes the world."[96]

---

92 "National," *Oxford Paperback Dictionary, Thesaurus, and Wordpower Guide*, 2001 ed.

93 "Nation," ibid.

94 "Race," ibid.

95 cf. Roxann Wheeler, *The Complexion of Race: Categories of Difference in Eighteenth-Century Britain* (Philadelphia: University of Pennsylvania Press, 2000) 237.

96 Thomas Hobbes, introduction, *Leviathan,* 1651 (12.11.2006 http://www.gutenberg.org/dirs/etext02/lvthn10.txt).

'Natural law' is part of a group of three connected ideological sources, the other two being 'Religion' and 'Humanitarianism'. In 18th-century discourse a person's natural rights are bound to infringe with religion, and religion again might not be clearly separable from what today would be called humanitarianism. In the present work, only arguments directly based on scripture are referred to as religious. Thus the difference between 'humanitarianism' and 'religion' can be established by stating that the latter is based directly on the Bible while the former is not, and thus rather depends on concepts of compassion and empathy. In this way also the difference between 'natural law' and 'humanitarianism' can be clarified. It goes without saying that while the first relies strongly on ideas of natural rights and state reason, and therefore on the works of philosophers such as Hobbes and Locke, the second is based on what could be called emotional truths such as compassion for ones fellow-beings, which I will explain in more depth in the next chapter.

### 3.3 Abolitionist Discourse as Sentimental Rhetoric

For a closer textual analysis of Clarkson's essays, I will use some elements of Brycchan Carey's approach to abolitionist discourse. In his *British Abolitionism and the Rhetoric of Sensibility* Carey argues that abolitionists used a very distinct sort of sentimental rhetoric. Through the use of certain sentimental tropes and arguments they tried to persuade their audiences of the slaves' suffering. By raising the readers' awareness of and pity for the suffering going on in Africa and the slave colonies they wanted to change their view and "to direct their opposition to it".[97] Carey states that sentimental rhetoric is part of the new rhetoric movement in which sensibility was seen as "a tap directly into the heart of the human condition".[98] In this way, emotion subverts intellect.

The notion of emotional truth is a romantic element in Clarkson's work. Therefore, part of the change in style in Clarkson's later work might be

---

[97] Brycchan Carey, *British Abolitionism and the Rhetoric of Sensibility: Writing Sentiment and Slavery* (Houndsmill and New York: Palgrave Macmillan, 2005) 2.
[98] ibid.

attributed to the emerging anti-romantic tendencies in the 19th century, also present for example in the works of Jane Austen.[99]

Carey states that Clarkson uses the familiar language of an 18th century sentimental novelist, apparent for example in his frequent use of words like 'Alas!'.[100] He sees Clarkson to be using two main sentimental arguments: the equality of feeling proves the equal status of all human beings and sympathy is a key motivating factor in human decision making.[101] Consequently the reader of the *Essay* is often asked to put himself in the slave's place. This technique rests on the Golden Rule, "Do to others what you would have them do to to you."[102]

Carey points out that in order to appeal to their readers' sympathy, abolitionist writers used several distinct sentimental rhetoric techniques. Such arguments against slavery that are "deduced from our own feelings and that divine sympathy, which nature has implanted in our breasts, for the most useful and generous of purposes" [103] are based on what Carey calls sentimental proof. This sort of proof is artificial, meaning not based on hard evidence but rather on rules as provided by logic, ethic or pathos. Sentimental proof relies heavily on the latter two.[104]

As mentioned above, Carey argues that the abolitionists' sentimental arguments are based on the Golden Rule and its assumption that all human beings experience pain and suffering in the same way which is a concept famously voiced, also in its racial implications, by Shylock in Shakespeare's *Merchant of Venice*: "Hath not a Jew eyes? [...] If you prick us, do we not bleed? If you tickle us do we not laugh? If you poison us, do we not die? ..."[105] Arguments

---

[99] cf. ibid 5.

[100] cf. ibid.
Query for keyword with AntConc in Clarkson's *Essay* (15.12.06 http://www.gutenberg.org/files/10611/10611-h/10611-h.htm ) 'alas!' used 13 times.

[101] cf. Carey, *The Rhetoric of Sensibility* 132.

[102] "Matthew 7;12" *The New Testament and Psalms: New International Version* (Lutherworth: The Gideons International, no year) 42.

[103] Clarkson, *Essay* 10 (Part 1, chap. I).

[104] cf. Carey, *The Rhetoric of Sensibility* 36f.

[105] cf. William Shakespeare, *The Merchant of Venice* (London: Oxford University Press, 1957). 203 (Act III, Scene I).

like this were "particularly useful to antislavery campaigners who faced a proslavery lobby who increasingly denied the humanity of Africans."[106]

A related technique is to reject false sensibility over trivial events or prompted by false reason. Although this seems not to be one of Clarkson's favourite techniques, elements of it can be traced in certain passages in which he refutes, or ironically deals with arguments of slave owners who hold that they act out of pity for the slaves, introducing Christianity and offering them better living conditions than they had had in Africa.[107]

These sentimental elements are part of the humanitarian side of Clarkson's arguments and will therefore be of importance for the humanitarian parameter of my analysis. Carey also suggests that Edward Said's model of Orientalism[108] can be adapted to describe abolitionist texts as constructing a similar sort of "Africanism."[109] Therefore I will also draw on some of Said's ideas in my interpretation of Clarkson's image of Africa and its inhabitants.

---

[106] Carey , *The Rhetoric of Sensibility* 38.
[107] cf. ibid. 38f.
[108] cf. Edward W: Said, *Orientalism* (New York: Vintage Books, 1979).
[109] Carey, *The Rhetoric of Sensibility* 4.

# 4 Critical Approach and Analysis

Three of Clarkson's essays form the basis of my further analysis:

- *An Essay on the Slavery and Commerce of the Human Species, Particularly the African, Translated from a Latin Dissertation, which was Honoured with the First Prize in the University of Cambridge, for the Year 1785, With Additions.* (1786); (referred to as: *Essay)*
- *An Essay on the Impolicy of the African Slave Trade. In Two Parts.* (1788); (referred to as: *Impolicy)*
- *Thoughts on the Necessity of Improving the Condition of the Slaves in the British Colonies, With a View to their Ultimate Emancipation; and on the Practicability, the Safety, and the Advantages of the Latter Measure.* (1823); (referred to as: *Thoughts)*

Where necessary I will also consult Clarkson's *History* on specific facts and details concerning Clarkson's biography and developments within the Society for Abolition during the years 1786 to 1807.

## 4.1 Clarkson's *Essay*

### *4.1.1 General Remarks*

In his history of the 'British Struggle to Abolish Slavery' Adam Hochschild speaks of the *Essay* as a curious document: "Heartfelt outrage glimmers through a certain mustiness of style."[110] And indeed, judging by today's scholarly standards, Clarkson's first essay is strange for the 21st century reader. I think Hochschild hits the point when he states that Clarkson had not yet quite shaken off the century he was living in.[111]

### *4.1.2 The Preface*

The first thing Clarkson describes in the preface of his *Essay* is how the Quakers in America abolished slavery among the members of their religious society. Although they expected this measure to be a considerable loss for them, Clarkson shows that "virtue seldom fails of obtaining its reward" and "became

---

[110] Hochschild 91.

[111] cf. Hochschild 91.

ultimately beneficial" because "most of the slaves returned without any solicitation to their former masters, to serve them at stated wages; as free men."[112] He adds that the work was done faster and better by free men and that the plantations were thus considerably more profitable.

Referring to the issue of labour discipline in this way will become a key argument in Clarkson's later work where his main aim seems not to be to remove the West Indian plantation system, but rather to create a more willing and thus more productive workforce. This, however, is the only passage of the *Essay* in which he mentions economic aspects of abolition. The reason for that might be that Clarkson wrote the introduction at a later time than the rest of the text, when he was more involved in the 'business' of professional abolitionism.

After telling the reader that the slave trade has long disgraced the "national character"[113] and, an inexhaustible mine of wealth is neglected in Africa, he introduces Granville Sharp and James Ramsay and their respective works. Then Clarkson deals with and refutes two apologist works on slavery, the *Cursory Remarks* on Ramsay's essay, and an *Apology for Negroe Slavery.* He mentions that the name of this "*cursory remarker* is Tobin."[114] This is the only time he actually tells the reader the name of an apologist writer. At all other times the pro-slavery side is simply referred to as "advocates for slavery"[115] and one time as "defenders of slavery."[116]

The last part of the introduction consists of Clarkson's account of how he came to translate and publish his *Essay*. He writes that he was "waited upon by some gentlemen of respectability and consequence who requested [him] to publish it in English"[117] and apologizes to the reader for the poor English style that resulted from the translation. Brycchan Carey identifies this as a *captatio*

---

[112] Clarkson, *Essay* 4 (Preface).

[113] ibid. 5 (Preface).

[114] ibid. 7 (Prefacc).

[115] Concordance query with AntConc in Clarkson's *Essay* (1.12.06 http://www.gutenberg.org/files/10611/10611-h/10611-h.htm ): 'advocates of slavery' used 5x.

[116] Clarkson, *Essay* 80 (Part 3, chap. IX).

[117] ibid. 8 (Preface).

*benevolenciae,* a rhetorical trope to ensure "the good will and attentive ears of the audience".[118]

This version of the publication history, however, is not consistent with the one in *History,* in which he writes that it was his own impulse to translate his dissertation.[119] Emphasizing the act of having been asked to translate the *Essay* possibly is Clarkson's way of conveying a modest picture of himself, in order to ensure the benevolence of the audience.

### *4.1.3 The Historical Dimension of Slavery in the Essay*

#### 4.1.3.1 The History of Slavery in Part I

The first part of the main text deals with the history of slavery. Clarkson's concept of this history is that "civilized, as well as barbarous nations, have been found, through a long succession of ages, uniformly to concur in the same customs."[120] For him these customs are both useful and "founded [...] on the principles of justice."[121] Slavery is described as one of the customs all nations develop at one point in their history. From this Clarkson deduces a possible pro-slavery argument, since the "force of custom pleads strongly" in favour of the "practice".[122] However, a humanitarian argument against slavery "seems immediately to arise in opposition of the former, deduced from our own feelings and that divine sympathy, which nature has implanted in our breasts".[123]

In the following portrayal of the history of slavery Clarkson divides slaves in "voluntary" and "involuntary".[124] The first class consists of persons who "had suffered the loss of liberty from their own imprudence"[125] such as debtors. He sees this kind of servitude as based on a contract and on the individual's choice of whether or not to engage with such practices that lead to servitude. It throws some light on Clarkson's concept of freedom, that he intends only to deal with

---

118 Carey, *The Rhetoric of Sensibility* 131.
119 cf. Clarkson, *History* 119 (chap. VII).
120 Clarkson, *Essay* 10 (Part 1, chap. 1).
121 ibid.
122 ibid.
123 ibid
124 ibid. 11 (Part 1, chap. I).
125 ibid.

the second class, "who were forced, without any such *condition* or *choice*, into a situation, which as it tended to degrade a part of the human species, and to class it with the brutal, must have been, of all human situations, the most wretched and insupportable."[126]

In his characteristic way of trying to bring taxonomical order to reality, he again divides the involuntary slaves into three classes: those who were publicly made slaves, such as prisoners of war, those who were "privately stolen in a state of innocence and peace"[127] and thus made slaves privately, and children who inherited their parents' state of bondage.

Looking at the history of slavery in classical times, Clarkson depicts the individual treatment of slaves in antiquity as being worthy of "our pity and abhorrence"[128] since the slaves were "beaten, starved, tortured, murdered at discretion; they were dead in a civil sense [...] were without appeal, [...] deprived of all possible protection, [and] without the possibility of redress."[129] Only in two places they were treated better: in Egypt and Athens, where quite moderate means of redress and protection for the slaves existed. In contrast to that it has to be noted that Clarkson adds: "we find all Eastern nations unanimous in the practice [of slavery]".[130]

The next chapter of the *Essay* is dedicated to the effects of the commerce of slaves. For Clarkson the fact that humans are treated like a commodity leads to barbarous and cruel treatment. Regarding them as brutes, and the brutal treatment itself, then lead to a depression of the slaves' mind and numb their faculties.[131] This is Clarkson's explanation for the notion of the slaves' inferiority. Thus, Clarkson reasons that slaves are not inferior by nature but by circumstance.[132] Still he maintains that slaves are inferior, albeit only because of the mutilation of their capacities by captivity.

---

[126] ibid. 10 (Part 1, chap. I).
[127] ibid. 15 (Part 1, chap. III)
[128] ibid. 16 (Part 1, chap. IV).
[129] ibid. 16 (Part 1, chap. IV).
[130] ibid. 12 (Part 1, chap. II)
[131] cf. ibid. 17/18 (Part 1, chap. V).
[132] cf. ibid. 18 (Part 1, chap. V).

Concerning slavery in Europe Clarkson explains that slavery upon its "full establishment"[133] was abolished not because of the establishment of the feudal system, which he obviously does not regard as a form of slavery, but because of the rise of Christianity.[134]

In sum, Clarkson sees the history of slavery as follows: after slavery in antiquity, Christianity led to a first abolition which lasted until "the Portuguese, within two centuries after its suppression in Europe, in imitation of those piracies, which we have shewn to have existed in the uncivilized ages of the world, made their descents on Africa, and committing depredations on the coast, first carried the wretched inhabitants into slavery."[135] Soon the other European nations started to partake in this trade, which Clarkson sees as "a melancholy instance of the depravity of human nature; as it shews, that neither the laws nor religion of any country, are sufficient to bind the consciences of some [...], who are ready to sacrifice their dearest principles at the shrine of gain."[136]

In Africa, the first consequence of the slave trade, as presented in the *Essay,* was that the natives fled from the shores and from the banks of the rivers. Thus, the Europeans were compelled to adopt a different system of procuring their human cargo: "They now formed to themselves the resolution of settling in the country; of securing themselves by fortified ports; of changing their system of force into that of pretended liberality; and of opening, by every species of bribery and corruption, a communication with the natives."[137] "The gaudy trappings of European art" [138] caught the attention of the African kings, who in turn took over the task of supplying slaves to the Europeans:

> A treaty of peace and commerce was immediately concluded: it was agreed, that the kings, on their part, should, from this period, sentence prisoners of war and convicts to European servitude; and that the Europeans should supply them, in return, with the luxuries of the north. This agreement immediately took place; and thus begun that commerce, which makes so considerable a figure at the present day.[139]

---

[133] ibid. 22 (Part 1, chap. VII)

[134] cf. ibid.

[135] ibid. 23/24 (Part 1, chap. VIII).

[136] ibid. 24 (Part 1, chap. VIII).

[137] ibid.

[138] ibid.

[139] ibid. 24/25 (Part 1, chap. VIII).

Clarkson analyses this as having led to a toppling of the social order, because the avarice of the kings, who had acquired a taste for luxuries, affected their justice:

> Not only those, who were fairly convicted of offences, were now sentenced to servitude, but even those who were suspected. New crimes were invented, that new punishments might succeed. [...]War was now made, not as formerly, from the motives of retaliation and defence, but for the sake of obtaining prisoners alone, and the advantages resulting from their sale.[140]

#### 4.1.3.2 The Use of the History and Image of Africa

From the above we can see that Clarkson's history of mankind is principally one of slavery. Therefore, he has to refute arguments based on the long tradition of slavery. The argument against slavery he develops from his historical account is that "there was no place so favourable to them [i.e. the slaves] as Athens"[141] and that also in Egypt "their condition [...] was more tolerable."[142] It is certainly no coincidence that Clarkson defends these two important sources of Western culture. The statement that the treatment of slaves in Egypt and Greece was better, connects culture and civilization with notions of freedom. By stating that all "Eastern nations"[143] unanimously were societies built on slave work he emphasises the historical division between orient and occident in which the 'West' is depicted as "rational, peaceful, liberal, logical, capable of holding real values [...],"[144] while the 'East' lacks all these qualities. Keeping slaves certainly fits the picture of a despotic orient.

Another interesting aspect is that Clarkson does not consider the European feudal system slavery, since it is governed by a contract. One could ask if there was actually much difference between the situations of a slave and a serf. Be that as it may, the European tradition of bound labour is defended by Clarkson, and we shall see later that the relationship between lord and serf is portrayed in a

---

140 ibid. 25 (Part 1, chap. VIII).

141 ibid. 16 (Part 1, chap. IV).

142 ibid.

143 ibid. 12 (Part 1, chap. II)

144 Said, *Orientalism* 49.

romantically positive way.[145] It would certainly be possible to depict West Indian slavery in a similar way, and this was actually done by proslavery authors.[146] Establishing the difference between a romantic, feudal, English past and the cruel situation in the West Indies, however, is an integral part of anti-slavery rhetoric. By means of a rather arbitrary geographical division forced labour in Africa and the West Indies is defined as slavery while European forms are not.

It is interesting that Clarkson sees the mere existence of slavery over long periods in human history to be an argument in favour of it. He refutes the overwhelming historical 'evidence' in favour of slavery by means of the religious paradigm. Temperley stresses that "until relatively recent times [...] Christian principles constituted a universal standard which it was incumbent upon all men to adopt."[147] Therefore pointing out that it was the introduction of Christian religion which led to the first abolition of slavery provides Clarkson with the decisive argument against what he calls "the force of custom."[148] Referring to this first abolition also serves Clarkson to depict his contemporary slavery as a complete anachronism.

The humanitarian and religious paradigms obviously weigh more heavily than historical tradition. It has to be observed that Clarkson is not opposed to forced labour per se. Apart from his defence of the feudal system, he makes it quite clear that also such persons who "suffered loss of liberty from their own imprudence"[149] do not deserve our pity as much as those who were made slaves involuntarily. Later on in the *Essay* he finds it acceptable that "civilized nations" employ their criminals for communal work such as the building of fortifications, roads, or for mining.[150]

---

[145] cf. David Brion Davis, "Abolitionism and Ideological Hegemony," *The Anti-slavery Debate: Capitalism and Abolitionism as a Problem in Historical Interpretation,* ed. Thomas Bender (Berkeley, Los Angeles and London: University of California Press, 1992) 168f.

[146] cf. Clarkson, Essay 45 (Part 2, chap. IX).

[147] Temperley, *Anti-Slavery as Cultural Imperialism* 336.

[148] Clarkson, *Essay* 10 (Part 2, chap. I)

[149]ibid. 11 (Part 1, chap.I)

[150] ibid. 43 (Part 1, chap. VIII)

The concept of nation is used in an interesting way in the *Essay*. Clarkson's frequent use of the words 'nation' and 'people'[151] shows that national categories are important for him. He mainly uses the national concept in connection with such attributes as 'different', 'civilized', and 'barbarous'.[152] This makes it evident that the concept of nation is often used in a contrastive way. Clarkson often refers to what 'civilized nations' do and to what 'barbaric nations' do. For example he states that "civilized, as well as barbarous nations, have been found, through a long succession of ages, uniformly to concur in the same customs [...]".[153] In an other place he backs an argument by stating that his "reasoning is true, and that civilized nations have considered it as such [...]".[154]

Clarkson's image of Africa is one of a country in the hands of "despotick sovereigns",[155] who sell their subjects to satisfy their own avarice. Later in the *Essay* he accuses the African kings of invading "the liberties of those, who, are in a state of *nature*, in a state of original *dissociation*, perfectly *independent*, perfectly *free*."[156] By doing so the sovereigns betray the trust put into them by society. This argument is of course based on John Locke's ideas about state reason.[157] Clarkson's logic also implies that the European traders, who disturbed the state of nature in the first place, share the guilt of initiating the trade with their African counterparts. Therefore the British nation, being more civilized, is the one to stop such a state of affairs. Such patterns of thought influenced later developments in Euro-African relations. As late as 1934 George M. Trevelyan writes in his *History of England* that "in Africa the slave trade and slavery had to be seen to an end" and that after the suppression of the slave trade in the

---

[151]Concordance query for words 'nation*' and 'people' (in the sense of ethinc group) with AntConc in Clarkson's *Essay* (23.11.2006, http://www.gutenberg.org/files/10611/10611-h/10611-h.htm ): 'nation*' used 43x and 'people' as collocating with 'black' 5x; 'white' 3x; 'civilized' 2x; 'different' 2x throughout the Essay and footnotes.

[152] Query for Collocations of 'nation*' with AntConc in Clarkson's *Essay* (23.11.2006, http://www.gutenberg.org/files/10611/10611-h/10611-h.htm) collocates with: 'different' 3x, 'civilized' 3x, and 'barbarous' 3x throughout Essay and footnotes.

[153] Clarkson, *Essay* 10 (Part 1, chap. I)

[154] ibid. 43 (Part 2, chap. VIII)

[155] ibid. 25 (Part 1, chap. VIII)

[156] ibid.

[157] cf. John Locke, *Two Treatises of Government: Of Civil-Government – Book II,* 1690 (16.08.2006 http://www.gutenberg.org/dirs/etext05/trgov10h.htm) chap. IV.

Viennese Congress "the British flag was closely connected with the freedom of the black race".[158] One can see how the liberation of the Africans can serve as a rationale to justify European involvement in Africa. David Brion Davis holds a similar view in his *Slavery and Human Progress,* when he states that antislavery ideology propagated that "the gradual eradication of coerced labour was synonymous with the material and moral progress of humanity as a whole and was the noblest mission and achievement of the nineteenth century."[159] In this way, "antislavery policies also sanctioned and extended British influence."[160] Also Seymour Drescher suggests a colonial dimension of abolitionism, pointing out that "antislavery was a legitimizer of imperialism before and after the fact."[161]

Clarkson's notion that the "state of nature"[162] is disturbed is based on a comparison with a European system of political state reason. John Locke provides him with the language to analyse what is wrong in the African kingdoms, and thus his main suggestions for improvement is the introduction of a European-like order. Clarkson's imposition of European ideas of state reason on native tribes in Africa can be seen in imperialist terms. Edward Said states in *Orientalism* that the analysis of other cultures is never value-free in the first place. Being able to analyse automatically implies one's own superiority. Such knowledge, as Clarkson claims to have of Africa, is to dominate it, to have authority over it.[163] Brycchan Carey suggests that abolitionists created a pseudo Africa, inhabited by pseudo Africans.[164]

So far three parameters have been applied to Clarkson's *Essay*: 'religion,' 'natural law,' and 'history'. Ideas of 'natural law 'and state reason are even more apparent in the next part of the *Essay*.

---

[158] George M. Trevelyan, *Geschichte Englands*, Vol.2 (München and Berlin: Oldenbourg, 1936) Vol 2, 678f (own translation).

[159] David Brion Davis, *Slavery and Human Progress* (New York and Oxford: Oxford University Press, 1986) 281.

[160] ibid.

[161] cf. Drescher, *Capitalism and Anti-slavery* 165.

[162] Clarkson, *Essay* 34 (Part 2, chap. V).

[163] cf. Said, *Orientalism* 32.

[164] cf. Carey, *The Rhetoric of Sensibility* 4.

### 4.1.4 *'Natural Law' and State Reason in Part II*

The aim of the second part of the *Essay* is to investigate in how far commerce and slavery of the human species are consistent with the laws of nature and the common notions of equity established among men.[165] Accordingly this part of the *Essay* is dedicated to a refutation of the concept of slavery on a very fundamental level. It is not so much a specific legal system Clarkson draws on to prove the wrongfulness of slavery, but rather the notion of certain natural rights that every human being should be granted. As the abolition of the slave trade certainly was an international issue, Clarkson wanted his work to be understood on such a level. Drawing on a specific national legal system would not have provided him with valid arguments for other European nations' fight against the slave trade, like the French or the Portuguese. Therefore Clarkson tries to find valid arguments for all slave trading nations.

His considerations about the "African Commerce, or Slave Trade"[166] are structured in the following way: first he deals with its wrongfulness on an individual level, then he turns to considerations of state reason, investigating the rights of the sovereign; finally he takes a look at the state's domination of the individual, using convicts and prisoners of war as examples.

#### 4.1.4.1 The Individual's Natural Rights

Clarkson's main premise is that mankind was originally free. As proof of this he refers to "divine writings",[167] fables, and ancient festivals which suggest an original freedom of mankind. The divine writings serve him to back up the point he wants to make. Clarkson mentions the *Saturnalian* carnival and "other similar festivals" as a "monument of this original equality of men".[168] He sees these festivals, in which "there was no rank, no distinction, no superior"[169] to be the remains of an original free human society. However, he does not seem to feel compelled to use the existence of an original free society to challenge the existing order, but rather acknowledges that the times of universal equality are

---

[165] cf. Clarkson, *Essay* 28 (Part 2, chap. I).
[166] ibid.
[167] ibid.
[168] ibid.
[169] ibid.

over, stating that we now live in "the third situation of mankind, a state of subordinate society".[170] In this way history, seen as a purposeful process, legitimates the present state of affairs.

Very selectively, Clarkson only takes his arguments against the trade of the human species from the alleged original equality of all men, and states that all property, by definition, has to be inferior to its owner. As an example he mentions the natural right of humans to rule over animals, due to the many "evident signs of the inferiority of their nature" [171] and to the fact that they are void of reason and thus not accountable for their actions. From this, Clarkson develops two arguments against slavery: firstly, that no man can be the property of another because all men are originally equal. Secondly, since men are to be held responsible for their actions, liberty cannot be something that is bought or sold:

> For if any one man can have an absolute property in the liberty of another, or, in other words, if he, who is called a master, can have a just right to command the actions of him, who is called a slave, it is evident that the latter cannot be accountable for those crimes, which the former may order him to commit. Now as every reasonable being is accountable for his actions, it is evident, that such a right cannot justly exist, and that human liberty, of course, is beyond the possibility either of sale or purchase.[172]

Clarkson distinguishes between interpersonal dominance and dominance by state or government. While he argues that one person can never be entitled to infringe with the accountability of another, he is careful not to question the state's right to impose its power on its subjects, as long as this is regulated by the social contract.

Clarkson then adds a justifying historical dimension to this idea of state reason by providing us with a history of the organization of human societies and forms of governments, divided into three periods. In the earliest times, he writes, men lived in a state of dissociation and independence. Then attacks by "fierce and rapacious beasts, [...] the predatory attempts of their own species, and the disputes of contiguous and independent families"[173] made it necessary to form a sort of society on the principles of preservation and defence. Clarkson explains

---

[170] ibid. 29 (Part 2, chap. I).
[171] ibid. 33 (Part 2, chap. IV).
[172] ibid.
[173] ibid. 28 (Part 2, chap. I).

these societies as still consisting of independent and free individuals living together without discipline or laws, rather like a herd, "doing, as a public body, what they had been accustomed to do as individuals before."[174] He calls this second stage of mankind the "state of independent societies".[175] The growth of population then made agriculture necessary as a means of subsistence, and with it an assignation of property took place. A form of government became necessary to "afford a security to the acquisitions of the industrious, and heal the intestine disorders of the community, by the introduction of laws".[176] Clarkson calls this third state of mankind, in which we still live, the "state of subordinate society".[177]

We can see again that he does not question the power relations of his contemporary society. The above explanations are strongly ideologically charged. He wants to show the reader the logic according to which the present society and its power relations emerged. Clarkson makes it quite clear that he opposes a change in the basic order of things since this would be against 'common sense'.

#### 4.1.4.2 The Sovereign's Rights and Obligations – State Reason

Turning to the question of the social contract binding the sovereign Clarkson expresses special dismay at the practice of some African rulers who sell their own subjects into slavery. To show that princes have no right to this, Clarkson reflects on early forms of government in chapter II. His starting point is to answer the question whether the introduction of government came about by compulsion, or by consent because, "when mankind first saw the necessity of government, it is probable that many had conceived the desire of ruling".[178] Taking for granted the original freedom and equality of all members of society, Clarkson explains that state power could never have been gained by force, but only by consent and for the mutual wealth of society. Therefore, the most wise,

[174] ibid. 29 (Part 2, chap. I)
[175] cf. ibid.
[176] ibid.
[177] cf. ibid.
[178] ibid. 30 (Part 2, chap. II).

prudent, just, and virtuous person became the leader and this title was not hereditary.

Clarkson's conclusion is that "liberty is a natural, and government is adventitious right, because all men were originally free."[179] In these arguments the influence of the English tradition of state philosophy is again quite obvious. In his discussion of slavery Locke wrote that "the natural liberty of man is to be free from any superior power on earth [and that] the liberty of man, in society, is to be under no other legislative power, but that established, by consent, in the commonwealth."[180] Where Locke calls the aim of government "commonwealth", Clarkson states that whether or not you view government as a contract, its aim certainly is the greatest possible happiness for the people.[181] And also Hobbes in his *Leviathan* sees the "wealth and the riches of all the particular members"[182] to be the strength of the political body. This is the foundation of what Clarkson believes to be 'natural law', as far as the sovereigns are concerned.

Thus it is obvious that the African prince, who publicly seizes his subjects, does not act in accordance with these legal principles. Therefore he has

> the voice of nature and justice against him. He breaks that law of nature, which ordains, 'that no just man shall be given into slavery, against his own consent:' he violates the first law of justice, as established among men, 'that no person shall do harm to another without a previous and sufficient provocation;' and he violates also the sacred condition of empire, made with his ancestors, and necessarily understood in every species of government, 'that, the power of the multitude being given up to the wisdom and justice of the prince, they may experience, in return, the most effectual protection from injury, the highest advantages of society, the greatest possible happiness.'[183]

Although Clarkson does not say so explicitly, the obvious consequence of a prince's failing to fulfil his part of the contract is that he forfeits his right to rule and can be rightfully removed from his office. Such ideas of state reason are one of the pillars on which Clarkson's arguing against the slave trade rests. A long term effect of such thought is that these arguments serve as a good rationale for European intervention in African domestic affairs. The slave-trading nations are

---

[179] ibid. 31 (Part 2, chap. III).

[180] Locke, *Two Treatises of Government.*

[181] cf. Clarkson, *Essay* 31 (Part 2, chap. III).

[182] Hobbes, *Introduction.*

[183] Clarkson, *Essay* 34 (Part 2, chap. V).

thus almost put under a moral obligation to remove African rulers and to see to it that the state reason they have disturbed is put into balance again.

#### 4.1.4.3 State and Individual – Convicts and POW

Clarkson's considerations of state reason have so far mainly been applied to the conduct of the "African princes."[184] However, he argues that what is true for the prince, must apply to an even higher degree for the common man who robs and sells his fellow creatures into slavery.

Having thus dealt with two of the three classes of slaves, those who are publicly seized and those who are privately kidnapped by individuals, he now moves on to the class of convicts who are sentenced to slavery and to prisoners of war. One of Clarkson's aims in writing about these two cases is to rule out the possibility of their use in arguments of the proslavery side.

He first tries to evaluate the punishment of convicts and POW and shows that African servitude is made up by elements of banishment, deprivation of liberty, and many corporal sufferings. His argument is that such a punishment is too severe for almost any possible crime. In addition, he emphasises that "such is the custom with the Africans: for, from the time, in which the Europeans first intoxicated the African princes with their foreign draughts, no crime has been committed, no shadow of a crime devised, that has not immediately been punished with *servitude*."[185] Furthermore, Clarkson is opposed to sentencing criminals to serve an other individual, for the state only has a just title to their labour. "Civilized nations"[186] let their delinquents only perform public work of national utility. "Because as the crimes they have committed are considered crimes against the public, no individual can justly receive the emoluments of their labour."[187]

This provides us with some insights into Clarkson's creed concerning the relationship between sovereign and individual. It strongly indicates that Clarkson was not opposed to forced labour per se, which was, as Drescher

---

[184] ibid. 36 (Part 2, chap. VI)
[185] ibid.
[186] ibid. 43 (Part 2, chap. VIII)
[187] ibid.

states, rather the norm than the exception in late $18^{th}$ century.[188] Clarkson contrasts the civilized European system of forced labour with the African and colonial practices. What disturbed him and other abolitionists was the arbitrariness with which slave traders and owners could practice their power over slaves. It was the lack of choice and of a regulating contract, as found in European forms of wage labour, that they stood up against in the first place. Clarkson's frequent protest against the fact that the slaves are "deprived of all possible protection"[189] and have to "suffer the bitterest of injuries without the possibility of redress"[190] give evidence to that.

The next chapter (VII) of Part 2 consists of Clarkson's discussion of the second possible exception, namely the legal status of prisoners of war. He starts out with his refusal of the ancient concept of the "right of capture",[191] stating that at war,

> when any of the contending parties had overcome their opponents, and were about to destroy them, the right was considered to commence; a right, which the victors conceived themselves to have, to recall their swords, and, from the consideration of having saved the lives of the vanquished, when they could have taken them by the laws of war, to commute *blood* for *service*.[192]

His argument against this runs as follows: it can only be lawful to kill out of necessity, but if someone is in a situation in which he can decide to spare his opponent, such necessity cannot exist at that moment. For Clarkson, Christianity is responsible that war was deprived of many of its former horrors, because the lives of the vanquished were spared out of conscientiousness.[193]

He goes on to refute arguments in favour of slavery drawing on principles of reparation and punishment. Citing Polybius, he elaborates that punishment does not apply since, by the laws of war, the participants have done nothing wrong as individuals. Public reparation must therefore not benefit or harm individuals, because it is the state, and not the individual soldier, that is offended in a war. Therefore, he concludes, if slavery can not be justified in a just war, even less so can it be in the unjust African wars in which "the African princes, corrupted by

---

[188] cf. Drescher, *Mighty Experiment* 19f.
[189] Clarkson, *Essay* 16 (Part 1, chap. IV)
[190] ibid.
[191] ibid. 37 (Part 2, chap. VII)
[192] ibid.
[193] cf. ibid. 38 (Part 2, chap. VII).

the merchants of Europe, seek every opportunity of quarrelling with one another [...]; and war is undertaken from no other consideration, than that of procuring slaves."[194] Clarkson took the concept of corrupt African kings from Anthony Benezet. It is striking, however, that where Benezet states that "*some* of the Negro rulers [are] corrupted by the Europeans,"[195] and spends some time discussing original African laws against robbery of humans, Clarkson tends to generalize more, and he presents all African rulers as corrupted tyrants.

It should by now be obvious that Clarkson's arguments are quite ambiguous. His 'natural-rights-based' arguments forbid single persons to dominate other individuals absolutely. His arguments of state reason, however, provide him with a language to force criminals to perform works of national benefit.

#### 4.1.4.4 Interim Results

I think it is time to draw some general conclusions from what I have dealt with so far. Since Clarkson never was in Africa he has to rely purely on second hand records to construct his picture of this huge continent. The outcome is that he builds a pseudo Africa inhabited by pseudo Africans, as Carey points out.[196] The information he works with is primarily such as has been recorded by Europeans. Hochschild states that "Clarkson and his colleagues had strikingly little interest in the testimony of any of the thousands of former slaves in Britain."[197] He claims to understand a continent to which he had never been, inhabited by people he had never met. Such a claim certainly shows elements of European superiority. His explanation model, that European corruption of the African princes is solely responsible for the state of affairs, is both oversimplifying and euro-centric, denying African ethnic groups autonomy. Therefore, his depiction of the African wars as irrational massacres, as terrible as they may have been, is the outcome of the small amount of one-sided information about the subject at his disposal. We can see that Clarkson, or the sources he draws on, desperately

---

[194] ibid. 39 (Part 2, chap. VII).

[195] Anthony Benezet, *Some Historical Account of Guinea, Its Situation, Produce, and the General Disposition of Its Inhabitants...*, 1771 and 1772 ( 18.08.2006 http://www.gutenberg.org/files/11489/11489-h/11489-h.htm#X)

[196] cf. Carey, *The Rhetoric of Sensibility.*

[197] Hochschild, *Bury the Chains* 133.

struggle to integrate the irritating and irrational reality, found on the 'dark continent', into European patterns of thought.[198] As I already mentioned above, Clarkson analyses the inner dynamics of 'his' Africa purely in terms of European state reason.

In sum two argumentative mainstays can be identified: on the one hand Clarkson argues against the slave trade by means of his considerations of state reason, human equality and justice which correspond to the ideological field of 'natural law'. Clarkson himself summarizes the point he wants to make: the commerce of slaves is beyond defence, "since it is contrary to the principles of *law* and *government*, the dictates of *reason*, the common maxims of *equity*, the laws of *nature*, the admonitions of *conscience*, and, in short, the whole doctrine of *natural religion*."[199] On the other hand the Essay, so far, has a strong historical dimension. I showed how Clarkson tends to glorify the European past and uses history to depict slavery as a gross antagonism. The emphasis changes at the end of Part II of the *Essay*.

### *4.1.5 Sentimental Rhetoric and Clarkson's Humanitarianism*

#### 4.1.5.1 African Wars and Arguments of the 'Purchasers'

To show the unjust practices of African despots in a more emotional way and to appeal to the readers' humanitarian feelings, chapter VIII of part 2 mainly consists of a quite dramatic account of one of the African skirmishes in which slaves are obtained. The origin of the account is not made clear in the *Essay*. Clarkson only writes that he quotes it from a writer "known to the author of the present Essay, who was a long time on the African coast".[200] Be it as it may, the narrator is on a ship on its way up an African river, when he sees "a numerous crowd approaching, with apparently little order, but in close array. They approach[...] very fast, and [fall] furiously on the inhabitants of the town [...] and both parties [fight] for about half an hour with the fiercest animosity [...]". The assailants finally get the better of the villagers pursuing them into the river, and "though they [have come] for the purpose of getting slaves, [give] no

---

[198]cf. Said, *Orientalism* 49.

[199] Clarkson, *Essay* 46 (Part 2, chap. IX).

[200] ibid. 44. (Part 2, chap. VIII - footnote).

quarter, their cruelty even prevailing over their avarice. They [make] no prisoners, but put all to the sword without mercy."[201] On this Clarkson only remarks that it shows that "every African war is a robbery".[202]

In the last chapter (IX) of the *Essay's* second part Clarkson deals with the arguments of those who purchase the slaves. He first states that even if the enslaving of convicts or other persons is lawful in an African society, this still does not change the intrinsic baseness of the practice, for laws cannot alter the nature of vice and the concerned persons are innocent in respect to the purchaser. This is one of the few instances where Clarkson refers to a specific legal system - "the laws of the Africans."[203] However, it goes without saying that for Clarkson his own moral considerations weigh more than the corrupt legal system of an African tribe.

He then turns to the purchasers' argument of buying prisoners of war to save them. He compares this with setting a man's house on fire (i.e. enticing the Africans to war) in order to save the inhabitants afterwards.[204] Clarkson also ridicules the argument that the Africans are taken "from their country for their own convenience",[205] because Africa, with its incessant heat, is unwholesome, and unfit to be inhabited. He argues that it is not appropriate in this case to judge from one's own feelings because the Africans are perfectly able to endure the climatic situation in their native country. This is a technique, which Brycchan Carey refers to as "rejection of false sensibility".[206]

#### 4.1.5.2 The Narrative of the 'Unhappy African'

One of the most frequently quoted parts of the *Essay*, in connection with an analysis of Clarkson's alleged sentimentality, is the narrative of the unhappy African, which serves as a more sentimental repetition of the different classes of slaves in the African trade. To help the reader imagine them, Clarkson makes up

---

[201] ibid. 41. (Part 2, chap. VIII).
[202] ibid. 42 (Part 2, chap. VIII).
[203] ibid. 45 (Part 2, chap. IX).
[204] cf. ibid.
[205] ibid.
[206] cf. Carey, *The Rhetoric of Sensibility* 39.

a scene in which a native, watching a "train of wretched slaves",[207] comments on the origin of the captives.

By today's academic standards the use of such a narrative in a scholarly essay is an uncommon technique. Clarkson's use of it gives evidence to Carey's view of sentimental rhetoric as being a popular rhetoric tool in 18th-century abolitionist discourse.

Clarkson tells us that the fictional scene he conjures up is in "agreement with unquestionable facts" and might therefore have happened just in the same way "had we been really there." [208] He takes us to an African village,

> And first, let us turn our eyes to the cloud of dust that is before us. It seems to advance rapidly, and, accompanied with dismal shrieks and yellings, to make the very air, that is above it, tremble as it rolls along. What can possibly be the cause? Let us inquire of that melancholy African, who seems to walk dejected near the shore; whose eyes are steadfastly fixed on the approaching object, and whose heart, if we can judge from the appearance of his countenance, must be greatly agitated.[209]

'Alas!' says the unhappy African, 'the cloud that you see approaching, is a train of wretched slaves. [....]'[210]

The nameless native, who is referred to at different times in the account as "the unhappy", "the melancholy", "the intelligent", and "the honest African",[211] then tells us that the slaves we see are about to be branded with a hot iron and will then be brought to the overseas colonies.[212]

However, the native, since he has learned the history of some of the unfortunate people we see, offers to tell us the "real causes of their servitude."[213] The point of view in the narrative is an interesting one. Using the first person plural, Clarkson has the reader stand next to him during the tale. First 'we' listen together with Clarkson, then 'we' answer the African.

What follows is a more emotional listing of the different classes of African slaves Clarkson has already mentioned in the preceding chapters of his *Essay*: the train of Africans Clarkson parades before 'us' consists of prisoners of war,

---

207 Clarkson, Essay 47 (Part 3, chap. I)

208 ibid.

209 ibid.

210 ibid.

211 ibid. 47f (Part 3, chap. I).

212 This is, however, not quite in accordance with the facts, for the slaves were not branded in Africa but only by their final owners in the colonies, a fact to which Clarkson only did justice in the second edition of his *Essay*.

213 Clarkson, *Essay* 47 (Part 3, chap. I).

convicts, of 'privately' kidnapped persons, and such individuals as were publicly seized by their despotic king. The last ones make up the biggest part. In an attempt to educate his audiences concerning the racial and national diversity of Africa, Clarkson lets the "honest African"[214] tell us about a certain group of slaves, "They speak a language, which no person in this part of Africa can understand, and their features, as you perceive, are so different from those of the rest, that they almost appear a distinct race of men. From this circumstance I recollect them."[215] And about how they came into servitude, he tells us:

> They are the subjects of a very distant prince, who agreed with the slave merchants, for a quantity of spirituous liquors, to furnish him with a stipulated number of slaves. He accordingly surrounded, and set fire to one of his own villages in the night, and seized these people, who were unfortunately the inhabitants, as they were escaping from the flames.[216]

The way he uses the European concept of nation to distinguish the different African tribes shows that Clarkson does not consider 'nation' as a man-made concept but rather treats it as a universal truth.

The captured Africans are sold to Christians, and the native concludes his narrative as follows,

> 'And now, as I have mentioned the name of Christians, a name, by which the Europeans distinguish themselves from us, I could wish to be informed of the meaning which such an appellation may convey. They consider themselves as men, but us unfortunate Africans, whom they term Heathens, as the beasts that serve us. But ah! how different is the fact! What is Christianity, but a system of murder and oppression? The cries and yells of the unfortunate people, who are now soon to embark for the regions of servitude, have already pierced my heart. Have you not heard me sigh, while we have been talking? Do you not see the tears that now trickle down my cheeks? and yet these hardened Christians are unable to be moved at all: nay, they will scourge them amidst their groans, and even smile, while they are torturing them to death. Happy, happy Heathenism! which can detest the vices of Christianity, and feel for the distresses of mankind.'[217]

'We' are shocked by such a notion of Christianity and 'we' immediately reply in an attempt to teach the naïve native a little lesson in religion:

> 'But' we reply, 'You are totally mistaken: Christianity is the most perfect and lovely of moral systems. It blesses even the hand of persecution itself, and returns good for evil. But the people against whom you so justly declaim; are not Christians. They are infidels. They are monsters. They are out of the common course of nature. Their countrymen at home are generous and brave. They support the sick, the lame, and

---

[214] ibid. 48 (Part 3, chap. I).

[215] ibid.

[216] ibid.

[217] ibid. 49 (Part 3, chap. I).

> the blind. They fly to the succour of the distressed. They have noble and stately buildings for the sole purpose of benevolence. They are in short, of all nations, the most remarkable for humanity and justice.'[218]

The cited passage seems to have two main rhetoric aims. Firstly, Clarkson tries to direct the audience's anger towards the damaging effect for the prestige of Christianity in Africa, drawing on their religious feelings. Secondly, he applies a sort of *'divide et impera'* strategy dividing the British public in two groups: the infidel and monstrous slave traders abroad and their countrymen at home in England, who are generous and brave. The sides Clarkson wants his audience to are quite obvious.

The constant use of 'we' forces the reader to adopt Clarkson's view. Together with him, 'we' speak: "Alas! Can the cries and groans with which the air now trembles, be heard across this extensive continent? Can the southern wind convey them to the ear of Britain? If they could reach the generous Englishman at home, [...] he would sympathize with you in your distress. He would be enraged at the conduct of his countrymen, and resist their tyranny."[219]

Looking at the train of captives "we indulged our imagination. We thought we beheld in one of them a father, in another an husband, and in another a son, each of whom was forced from his various and tender connections, and without even the opportunity of bidding them adieu." [220] Such passages are possibly aimed at the increasingly industrialised and urbanized inhabitants of industrial towns in the North of England, who might have drawn parallels to their own experience of the destruction of the nuclear family. In his *History* Clarkson points out that he was especially welcomed in the industrial town of Manchester.[221] Drescher states that "the corruption of this primary human organization remained one of the most enduring indictments against the slave system."[222]

#### 4.1.5.3 The Middle Passage and the Conditions in the West Indies

---

[218] ibid.

[219] ibid. 50 (Part 3, chap. I).

[220] ibid. 49 (Part 3, chap. I).

[221] cf. Clarkson, *History* 201f (chap. XIX)

[222] cf. Drescher, *Anti-slavery and Capitalism 163/164.*

After the passage with the African's tale, Clarkson turns to the middle passage and the treatment of the slaves at their final destination, the West Indian sugar colonies.

In order to prove the unbearable conditions during the passage, Clarkson mentions the high mortality rate of 20,000 slaves per year due to poor hygienic conditions, punishment for mutiny, and suicide. He then tell us that sometimes the human cargo is jettisoned for want of provisions, or in order to betray insurance companies. Clarkson concludes this chapter by remarking again on the splitting up of families and by mentioning "an instance of wanton, barbarity, which happened some time ago." He quotes a gentleman, who "is at present resident in England [... and is ] a person of the strictest integrity, and who was at the time in the place where the transaction happened."[223] What follows is the depiction of an officer on a Guinea ship brutally beating up, and finally killing a slave in public on a West Indian Island. Clarkson concludes that even cattle is better protected in England than slaves in the colonies.

He then "takes [his] leave of the first receivers"[224] and goes on to deal with the treatment of the slaves on the plantations. He contrasts their work as beasts of labour with the life they led in their own countries, "a life of indolence and ease, where the earth brings forth spontaneously the comforts of life, and spares frequently the toil and trouble of cultivation."[225] This shows the simplified, idyllic picture Clarkson has of the African continent again.

He states that during the first two years three out of four slaves die, which in the planters jargon is called the seasoning. Clarkson's depiction of the working conditions is often quite dramatic. He shows the reader that the slaves lead a life of "unparalleled drudgery",[226] and are not even "comfortably clothed, and plentifully fed".[227] During harvest time they work sixteen hours a day in the fields for their master and are "employed three [hours] afterwards in their own necessary concerns;"[228] therefore, only three hours of sleep are left for them.

---

223 Clarkson, *Essay* 51/52 (Part 3, chap. II).
224 ibid. 52 (Part 3, chap. II).
225 ibid. 53 (Part 3, chap. IV).
226 ibid. 54 (Part 3, chap. IV).
227 ibid.
228 ibid.

During the rest of the year, in addition to the field work, also the mills have to be worked twenty-four hours a day, and those who are too tired and "feed the mill between asleep and awake, suffer, for obeying the call of nature, by the loss of a limb."[229]

To ensure the reader's attention and sympathy for the sufferers, Clarkson describes the slaves' punishment with incredible intensity and vividness: the constant use of the whip, which "erases the skin, and cuts out small portions of the flesh at almost every stroke and is so frequently applied, that the smack of it is all day long in the ears of those, who are in the vicinity of the plantations."[230] Diabolical ingenuity is used to contrive new modes of torture:

> An iron coffin, with holes in it, was kept by a certain colonist, as an auxiliary to the lash. In this the poor victim of the master's resentment was inclosed, and placed sufficiently near a fire, to occasion extreme pain, and consequently shrieks and groans, until the revenge of the master was satiated, without any other inconvenience on his part, than a temporary suspension of the slave's labour. Had he been flogged to death, or his limbs mutilated, the interest of the brutal tyrant would have suffered a more irreparable loss.[231]

Clarkson admits that this goes beyond the day-to-day cruelty against slaves but holds that it is a good example for the corrupting effect the practice of slavery has not only on its victims but also on their owners, "while it hardens their hearts, and makes them insensible of the misery of their fellow-creatures, it begets a turn for wanton cruelty."[232] The effect on the slaves is shown to be a two-sided one. Some of them flee from their masters, which makes them outlaws who are 'wanted dead or alive'. Presenting their cut-off heads, still reeking with blood, as a trophy was the proof required by law to entitle their captors to their reward. Other slaves, "so deeply pierced by the excruciating fangs of hunger, as almost to be driven to despair, are driven to steal food or to eat some of the sugar cane they plant and harvest. Clarkson vividly shows the consequence of such 'crimes':

> [...]the smart of the whip has not been the only pain that the wretched Africans have experienced. Any thing that passion could seize, and convert into an instrument of punishment, has been used; and, horrid to relate! the very knife has not been

---

229 ibid.

230 ibid. 55 (Part 3, chap. IV).

231 ibid.

232 ibid.

> overlooked in the fit of phrenzy. Ears have been slit, eyes have been beaten out, and bones have been broken;[233]

We can see that Clarkson's depiction of plantation life in the *Essay* is mainly characterized by passages about the suffering of the slaves. The chapter ends with a quite declamatory appeal to King Alfred the Great:

> Immortal Alfred! father of our invaluable constitution! parent of the civil blessings we enjoy! how ought thy laws to excite our love and veneration, who hast forbidden us, thy posterity, to tremble at the frown of tyrants! how ought they to perpetuate thy name, as venerable, to the remotest ages, who has secured, even to the meanest servant, a fair and impartial trial! How much does nature approve thy laws, as consistent with her own feelings, while she absolutely turns pale, trembles, and recoils, at the institutions of these receivers![234]

This invocation of the father of the British constitution serves Clarkson to distinguish clearly between the lawless state of affairs in the colonies, and the ordered legal situation at home. This shows that one of the abolitionists' aims certainly was to 'export' British standards to the colonies, part of which was the concept of wage labour. It is one of Seymour Drescher's assumptions that the spread of the free-labour ideology was an integral part of what he calls "the mighty experiment".[235]

In the following chapter of his *Essay* Clarkson explains why self-interest of the planters does not keep their cruelty against their slaves in check. Firstly, "self-interest will be found but a weak barrier against the sallies of passion, particularly where it has been daily indulged in its greatest latitude, and there are no laws to restrain its calamitous effects."[236] An other thing that makes the planters prone to severity and cruelty is an interest of self-preservation, which "demands the most rigorous severity. For when we consider that where there is one master, there are fifty slaves [who are] perpetually at war in their hearts with their oppressors, and [...] continually cherishing the seeds of revenge."[237] The resulting danger for their lives compels the masters to "adopt a system of tyranny and oppression".[238]

---

[233] ibid. 56 (Part 3, chap. IV).
[234] ibid. 57 (Part 3, chap. IV).
[235] cf. Drescher, *Mighty Experiment* 19ff.
[236] Clarkson, *Essay* 59 (Part 3, chap. V).
[237] ibid.
[238] ibid.

Clarkson's logic here is not consistent with what he writes in his later work. In the *Essay* a system of oppression is shown to be the only way of keeping the slaves in check and from returning to their homelands. In *Thoughts*, on the other hand, treating slaves more leniently is what Clarkson recommends as a first step to their emancipation; great part of this work consists of his explanations as to why such a step would not only be without danger, but even profitable for the planters.

In a short sixth chapter Clarkson laments on the sinfulness of placing the slaves in the colonies in a position to either steal or perish. He consequently acknowledges the right of the slaves to rebel in such a situation to get their natural freedom back from owners who have no title over their persons. After that he starts to refute the argument that Africans "are an inferior link of the chain of nature, and are made for slavery."[239] This poses a thematic break, and therefore I will try to draw some conclusions before dealing with the last chapters of the *Essay.*

#### 4.1.5.4 Sentimental Rhetoric and Humanitarianism

Clarkson's humanitarian arguments are mostly presented in a way to stir the reader's humanitarian and pitiful feelings. He tries to appeal to the audiences' own feelings and experiences and urges the reader to put himself in the place of the suffering Africans. The fact that throughout the *Essay* Clarkson continually uses adjectives such as "unfortunate," "wretched", "unhappy", or "poor"[240] when referring to Africans, indicates what sort of feelings he wants to raise among his readers.

Carey argues that "during the middle to late eighteenth century, many writers and public speakers used a distinct and recognisable sentimental rhetoric, and that participants in the abolition debate used this rhetoric particularly extensively.[...] Central to the rhetoric is a belief in the power of sympathy to raise awareness of suffering, to change an audience's view of that suffering, and

---

[239] ibid. 61 (Part 3, chap. IV).

[240] Query for keywords in Clarkson's *Essay* (1.11.2006, http://www.gutenberg.org/files/10611/10611-h/10611-h.htm): 'unfortunate' used 43x, 'wretched' used 27x, 'unhappy' used 11x, and 'poor' used 5x in connection with slaves or Africans.

to direct their opposition to it."[241] Sentimental authors saw this sort of rhetoric as a "powerful rhetoric tool [...] to tap directly into the heart of the human condition."[242] The first instance of this kind of rhetoric can already be found at the beginning of part one, where Clarkson weighs the fact that slavery has a long history in all cultures, which "pleads strongly on the one hand [i.e. in favour of slavery],"[243] against the natural feelings of pity for the suffering of fellow creatures and decides in favour of the latter. In connection with his discussion of the African convicts he offers a very sentimental explanation as to why banishment is such a severe punishment. Drawing on the reader's own feelings of home and childhood he argues that "What must be their sufferings to be forced for ever from the country? Which contains the spot, in which they were born and nurtured; which contains their relations and friends [...]".[244] It is obvious that he wants the reader to imagine himself in a similar situation and to feel pity for the suffering Africans.

Also the war scene in the African village is aimed at raising the reader's sympathy for the poor Africans when "Women and children of the town were clustered together at the water's edge, running shrieking up and down with terror. [While the attackers] were continually dragging out and murdering those, whom by reason of their wounds they easily overtook. [And even] the very children whom they took in great numbers, did not escape the massacre".[245] Seymour Drescher, quite plausibly, suggests that such a depiction of the violent uprooting of African villages and the destruction of human networks had special resonance in the industrial North of England, which experienced a roughly similar process.[246] The tale of the unnamed African again appeals to notions of family and home. In the end Clarkson even asks the reader to see the train of slaves as consisting of fathers, sons, husbands etc. "each of whom was forced

[241] Carey, *The Rhetoric of Sensibility* 1/2.
[242] ibid. 2.
[243] Clarkson, *Essay* 10 (Part 1, chap. I)
[244] ibid. 36 (Part 2, chap. VI).
[245] ibid. 41 (Part 2, chap. VIII).
[246] cf. Drescher, *Capitalism and Anti-slavery* 163.

from his various and tender connections, and without even the opportunity of bidding them adieu."[247]

On the other hand he also tries to establish a contrast between civilized and lawful Britain and the situation in Africa by depicting the Englishmen at home as generous and sympathizing and the slave traders abroad as infidel monsters.[248] The narrative is a technique Carey refers to as sentimental parable; a short story with a moral serves to illustrate an otherwise complicated situation.[249] Although Clarkson claims that the African's narrative is strictly consistent with fact, it still remains a piece of fiction. Therefore, the facts lose some of their importance to put more emphasis on ethics and moral. Carey mentions that further typical features of the sentimental parable are that it mostly deals with some form of suffering, that a benevolent and philanthropic moral is drawn and that often the suffering of an individual, who is given a name, stands for the suffering of a group. The aim is to offer the audience a face with which to associate suffering, and thus to form a personal relationship between reader and sufferer. I have already suggested a similar sort of personal connection concerning the parallels between the changes affecting the working classes in the North of England in the process of industrialisation and urbanization, and the violent uprooting of family bonds and other human networks in Africa.[250]

While generally the narrators of sentimental narratives are given a name to make them more personal, it is striking that Africans very often have to do without a name.[251] Clarkson, never having been to Africa, cannot come up with a true individual but has to resort to stereotypes to make his point. The column of nameless Africans paraded before the reader are therefore a piece of Africanist discourse.[252]

As I have already mentioned, another strategy of sentimental rhetoric is to accuse one's adversary of false sensibility. This is what Clarkson does in the last

---

[247] Clarkson, *Essay* 48 (Part 3, chap.I)

[248] cf. ibid. 49 (Part 3, chap.I)

[249] cf. Carey, *The Rhetoric of Sensibility* 39f

[250] cf. Drescher, *Capitalism and Anti-slavery* 163.

[251] cf. ibid.

[252] cf. ibid. 132/133.

passage of part II, in which he rejects pseudo-humanitarian arguments of the proslavery side, like 'saving' the Africans from their wretched country.[253]

A further sentimental feature of Clarkson's work is emotional subversion of the intellect. This is a technique that works in two ways. On the one hand, rational arguments can be devalued by appealing to the reader's emotions. And on the other hand, which is very often the case with Clarkson, intellectual arguments are enhanced by referring to the fact that the reader's feelings point in a similar direction. This technique can be observed on all levels of the *Essay*. Even the large-scale structure of the *Essay* can be described in these terms. Clarkson begins with the history of slavery and explains why it is contrary to the concept of 'natural law.' This is followed by the more sentimental part with the narratives and accounts about Africa and the West Indies trying to make the reader not only understand but also to feel Clarkson's point.

Clarkson's conclusion is that only the unawareness of the English public is responsible for what is going on in the African trade. Starting a process of public enlightenment with his writing, and causing a passionate public outcry, is the solution to the problem for him. In order to reach that aim, it is important to connect with the audience in a proper way, hence the use of sentimental techniques to tap into the hearts of the English public. Thus sentimental rhetoric is an important part of Clarkson's humanitarian arguments. Especially those passages in which he refers to the suffering of African families, women, or children are different from his religiously motivated arguments.

### *4.1.6 Concepts of Race in the Essay*

In chapters VII and VIII of the *Essay's* third part, Clarkson deals with "that other system of reasoning which is always applied, when the former is confuted; 'that the Africans are an inferior link of the chain of nature, and are made for slavery.'"[254] He names two pro-slavery arguments: firstly, that the Africans are made for slavery due to their alleged inferiority of capacities and, secondly, because of their "colour, and [...] those other marks, which distinguish them

[253] cf. Carey, *The Rhetoric of Sensibility* 39.

[254] Clarkson, *Essay* 61 (Part 3, chap. VII).

from the inhabitants of Europe."[255] Again Clarkson's reference to the proslavery side is quite vague. He does not tell the reader where he takes these arguments from. They are presented as if they were common knowledge. It is a curious fact that pro-slavery writers did actually not rely on racial arguments to such a degree as Clarkson suggests in the *Essay*. Peter Kitson argues that Clarkson emphasizes the importance of race to a degree that is not justified by the actual status of racist arguments in proslavery counter arguments.[256]

The following part of the *Essay* shows some of the prevailing forms of racism in Clarkson's days: in the same way in which he tries to bring Linnaean order to complicated historical facts, he also tries to subject human variation to this sort of hierarchical order. Clarkson uses Genesis as proof that all humans have one common origin. Therefore, Clarkson certainly has to be seen as a monogenist. However, the existing phenotypic diversity seems to worry him sufficiently to dedicate a quite substantial part of the *Essay* to consider the variation of human appearance. Phillip Curtin sees the Linnaean system of classification and the belief that God or Nature has organised all creation in a great, hierarchical "Chain of Being" [257] as having provided the theoretical underpinning for a similar racial classification of man.[258] I have pointed out before that the hierarchical structure in which Clarkson orders fact suggests that he was probably well acquainted with Linnaeus's work.

Clarkson first aims at a clarification of the proslavery lobby's alleged arguments. Concerning the slaves' abilities and talents he admits – as already done in the part of the *Essay* dealing with the history of slavery - that the colonial slaves are indeed of inferior faculties. The reason for that, however, is only the cruel treatment they are subjected to. Consequently their minds, "depressed by rigorous servitude, cannot be excited to a display of those

[255] ibid. 66 (Part 3, chap. VII).

[256] cf. Peter Kitson, "'Candid Reflections': The Idea of Race in the Debate over the Slave Trade and Slavery in the Late Eighteenth and Early Nineteenth Century," *Discourses of Slavery and Abolition: Britain and its Colonies, 1760-1838*, eds. Brycchan Carey, Markman Ellis, and Sara Salih (Houndsmill and New York: Palgrave Macmillan, 2004) 11.

[257] Philip Curtin, "The Africans' 'Place in Nature,'" *Racism*, eds. Martin Bulmer, and John Solomos (Oxford: University Press, 1999) 33.

[258] cf. ibid.

faculties, which might otherwise have shone with the brightest lustre."[259] That is followed by a quite interesting passage in which Clarkson shows his views on how the abilities of men are awakened. For him the principle of hope and reward is what exerts the mind's faculties and brings them to public view. Slaves, however, have no hope but "that their miseries will be soon terminated by death."[260]

At this point Clarkson's deliberations start to show racist elements. He sets out to deal with the talents and failings of 'the African people' in general, applying a racially based concepts of nation and culture. Trying to form a "true judgment of the abilities of these unfortunate people,"[261] he acknowledges the obviously racist assumption that there is such a thing as a distinguished racial character with certain abilities or failings common to all members of an ethnic group. In forming his judgement he allows race to be a distinctive feature, which is what racism is about. Bulmer and Solomos define racism as a belief that a designated racial group is either biologically or culturally inferior and also as using such a belief to rationalize the racial group's treatment in society.[262]

While he goes at quite some length to refute the African's biological inferiority, the assumption of their cultural inferiority, albeit due to oppression by European slave traders and other circumstances, remains. As I have shown above, Clarkson assesses 'the Africans' to be culturally less developed than 'the Europeans.' The second part of Bulmer and Solomos' definition fits Clarkson's work even more. In accusing the defenders of the slave trade to justify the practice on racial grounds, he explains an existing social condition by racial difference. His assumption in this part of the *Essay* is that race after all is one of the reasons why the Africans are used as slaves.

Then Clarkson explains the African culture before the commencement of slavery, and he takes a look at those Africans who "had any opportunity [...] of shewing their genius either in arts or letters."[263] He states that the Africans still

---

[259] Clarkson, *Essay* 62 (Part 3, chap. VII).

[260] ibid.

[261] ibid.

[262] Martin Bulmer and John Solomos, introduction, *Racism,* eds. Martin Bulmer & Sohn Solomos (Oxford: University Press, 1999) 4.

[263] Clarkson, *Essay* 63 (Part 3, chap. VII).

live in a savage state on their native soil and "follow the same mode of life, and exercise the same arts, as the ancestors of those very Europeans, who boast their great superiority, are described to have done in the same uncultivated state [sic!]."[264] Here we see again that he describes the Africans to be on a lower level of development than the Europeans. Clarkson draws three conclusions from his survey of African accomplishments, "that their abilities are sufficient for their situation;-that they are as great, as those of other people have been, in the same stage of society;-and that they are as great as those of any civilized people whatever, when the degree of the barbarism of the one is drawn into a comparison with that of the civilization of the other."[265]

Such arguments can justify the interventions of 'benevolent' colonial powers wanting to 'help' the barbarous savages with the blessings of European achievements, and make the act of doing so even virtuous. I have already shown above that some scholars see antislavery as having provided a better channel for European influence in Africa than slave trade did.[266]

After that Clarkson discusses the Africans' abilities in different fields of employment, always remembering that "even their most polished situation may be called barbarous, and that this circumstance, should they appear less docile than others, may be considered as a sufficient answer to any objection that may be made to their capacities."[267] Concerning their ingenuity in mechanical arts he states that "they do not discover a want" and "attain them in as short a time as the Europeans, and arrive at a degree of excellence equal to that of their teachers."[268] He regards the Africans' performance in liberal arts as less proficient; "but not less in proportion to their time and opportunity of study."[269] Their abilities in music are commonly acknowledged, since some of their tunes have even been imported to England. And he also makes a point that the Africans exhibit a conspicuous talent for poetry, because "every occurrence, if

[264] ibid. 62 (Part 3, chap. VII).
[265] ibid. 63 (Part 3, chap. VII).
[266] cf. Davis, *Slavery and 'Progress'* 363.
[267] Clarkson, *Essay* 63 (Part 3, chap. VII).
[268] ibid.
[269] ibid.

their spirits are not too greatly depressed, is turned into a song."[270] He dismisses critique of the slaves' poems regarding them as incoherent and nonsensical on grounds of the Africans' poor knowledge of the English language (obviously he is talking about those Africans who have already been made slaves in the colonies), and their "wildness of thought, arising from the different manner, in which the organs of rude and civilized people will be struck by the same object."[271]

It can be stated by now that Clarkson's general assessment of native Africans is one of rude, uncivilized savages. Nevertheless, he sees a possibility for development. Once the impediments of uncivilized life have been removed and the uncivilized African has received an education, all his "defects"[272] vanish. To back this hypothesis he quotes from two poems by Phillis Wheatley: "Hymn to the Morning" and "Thoughts on Imagination". It is striking that Wheatley is not referred to by her name in the *Essay*. It is only in a footnote that we are told the name of the author "Phillis Wheatley, Negro slave to Mr. John Wheatley, of Boston in New England", and even there she has to share the space with her white owner. Together with the prose compositions of Ignatius Sancho, Clarkson thinks this to be sufficient proof for African literary capacities.

Judging from this, Clarkson's concept of the African race, so far, is a culturally defined one. In his *Essay* he tries to minimize the effects of race on people's character and abilities. Instead of race as such, however, he uses geographical and historical distinctions in order to explain why the peoples of Africa, although potentially equal to Europeans, are so different. These terms of description become even more obvious in his discussion of skin colour in chapter VIII. This is the part of Clarkson's writings which is most frequently quoted in connection with a discussion of abolitionist racism. In this chapter Clarkson tries to refute the argument that black skin colour and other bodily markers designate Africans for being slaves to white Europeans.

First of all, three arguments based on colour are again presented as being used by the advocates of the slave trade to legitimise it. The two first mentioned are

---

[270] ibid.

[271] ibid.

[272] ibid. 63 (Part 3, chap. VII).

derived from interpretations of the Old Testament. They build upon the scriptural 'fact' that Africans are descended either from Cain or from Ham. In both cases the Bible would, by "divine inspiration",[273] justify that they should be servants to the rest of the world. The first of these two versions (i.e. the Africans as descendants from Cain) is dismissed by Clarkson with only two sentences: "If the scriptures are true, it is evident that the posterity of Cain were extinguished in the flood. Thus one of the arguments is no more."[274] The second version, holding that the curse of Ham made his descendants slaves, takes Clarkson a bit longer to dismiss on scriptural grounds, but in the end he reaches the conclusion that "the second argument is wholly inapplicable and false [...], as the curse has been long completed."[275]

More interesting, in racial terms, is the third argument, in which the Africans are described "as a totally distinct species of men," and the ones using it "conclude them [i.e. the Africans] to be an inferior link of the chain of nature, and deduce the inference described."[276]

The rest of the chapter is taken up by Clarkson's discussion of this argument, in both religious terms and from a scientific point of view. Throughout he attempts to form a synthesis of these two seemingly contrary approaches.

It is quite remarkable that he dismisses the general notion to justify slavery purely by outer appearance. If this were just, he argues, then the British would have a right to enslave the inhabitants of Spain or France, which is "too ridiculous to be farther noticed."[277] If the difference in colour is indeed so ridiculous, the question why Clarkson discusses the topic at such length in the *Essay* has to be raised. Obviously, complexion is not so irrelevant for him after all.

Then Clarkson proves that all humans are of one species. This is a fact, because "it is an universal law, that if two animals of a different species propagate, their offspring is unable to continue its own species."[278] The divine reason for this is,

---

[273] Clarkson, *Essay* 66 (Part 3, chap. VIII).
[274] ibid.
[275] ibid. 67 (Part 3, chap. VIII).
[276] ibid. 66 (Part 3, chap. VIII).
[277] ibid. 68 (Part 3, chap. VIII).
[278] ibid.

that it "prevents the world form being overrun by monsters."[279] However, "the mulattoe is as capable of continuing his own species as his father."[280] Clarkson identifies this as a proof for the correctness of the Bible, and that "God, who hath made the world, hath made of one blood all the nations of men that dwell on all the face of the earth." [281]

A semi-scientific and semi-religious explanation that all mankind must originally have been of one colour, since all are the descendents of Noah, follows. The original colour of mankind was the same sort of dark olive, which is still found today in the country where Noah and his sons lived. Also in the following discussion of how the variation of skin colour around the world came about, Clarkson uses the Bible as a historical source. He deduces two possible epochs in which the difference of colour might have been produced by Divine interposition. He dismisses the first, concerning the curse of the posterity of Ham, on scriptural grounds. He also disregards a second version, according to which different colours were introduced to assist the confusion of language, when the tower of Babel was built: since it cannot account for "that regular gradation of colour from the equator to the poles, so conspicuous at the present day."[282] His inference therefore is that it was not direct divine interposition at all that caused the variations of skin colour of the human species, but rather an "incidental co-operation of causes."[283]

According to Clarkson the place where skin colour is located is the "mucosum corpus,"[284] which lies underneath the cuticle, the transparent upper surface of the skin. Climate is responsible for bringing about the different complexions. Clarkson even explains the fact that not all "people under the same parallels are exactly of the same colour."[285] Such climatic influences as the cooling effects of "high mountains in the neighbourhood", "spreading succulent plants" affording "agreeable cooling shades" or the heating effect of the proximity of "burning

---

[279] ibid.
[280] ibid.
[281] ibid.
[282] ibid. 69 (Part 3, chap. VIII).
[283] ibid.
[284] ibid. 70 (Part 3, chap. VIII).
[285] ibid. 71 (Part 3, chap. VIII).

sands and sulphurous metallick particles [...] exhaling from the bowels of the earth"[286] account for further differences in colour.

Some examples are to give further evidence to this theory. Clarkson calls it an "incontrovertible fact [...] that when black inhabitants of Africa are transplanted to colder, or the white inhabitants of Europe to hotter climate, their children, born there, are of a different colour of themselves; that is lighter in the first, and darker in the second instance."[287] In the first instance he, perhaps a bit naively, underestimates the genetic influence of the white planters in the colonies, who sexually exploited and impregnated their female slaves. The second 'fact' he uses to give evidence to his theory, is a purely arbitrary one. He writes that, "*the children of the blackest Africans are born white.* In this state they continue for about a month, when they change to a pale yellow. In process of time they become brown. Their skin still continues to increase in darkness with their age, till it becomes of a dirty, sallow black, and at length, after a certain period of years, glossy and shining."[288] This statement is quite confusing. Apart from its blatant inconsistency with reality, one has to ask why Clarkson first insists on the original colour of mankind being a dark olive, only to announce now that the colour of all new-borns around the world is white. Concepts of the colour white as indicating purity might be responsible for this sentiment. The passage again shows that colour does matter to Clarkson after all. If it really was "too ridiculous to be farther noticed,"[289] there would be no need to deal with the issue of complexion in such depth.

As a third example he explains the different complexions that can be found among European Jews. Climate's influence can be most strikingly observed in them, since "they have preserved themselves distinct from the rest of the world by their religion; and, [...] they never intermarry with any but those of their own sect, [...] they have no mixture of blood in their veins."[290] Therefore the fact that the English Jew is white, the Portuguese swarthy, the Armenian olive, and the Arabian copper can only be attributed to the influence of climate, according to

[286] ibid.
[287] ibid. 72 (Part 3, chap. VIII).
[288] ibid.
[289] ibid. 68 (Part 3, chap. VIII).
[290] ibid. 73 (Part 3, chap. VIII).

Clarkson. The use of this example shows the degree to which Clarkson embraces, what would today be called, racist concepts, struggling to define a religious group by biological means.

Before he concludes his chapter with a summary of his main points, the reader is confronted with further anatomical reflections on the origin of skin colour. Here Clarkson develops a concept of blackness as a sort of universal freckle. From the drying out of the accumulating fluid in the mucous substance of the body, the liquids in the skin become thicker and deeper coloured, due to heat.[291]

Clarkson concludes the chapter by stating that Negroes cannot be made for slavery. If they were, there would be evident signs of their inferior nature, which cannot be found. The existing differences are only due to the fact they are adapted to their environmental circumstances. Thus Clarkson, while asserting morphological differences, does not use them as markers of inferiority. What he does imply, however, is a notion that Africans are certainly better suited to work in the hot areas of the world than Europeans.

#### 4.1.6.1 The Racial Paradigm

I have already remarked on Clarkson's tendency to impose scientific and hierarchical order on the complexity of reality, and how these concepts are linked to the emergence of racism. George Mosse writes that "modern racism had its origins in Enlightenment and in a religious revival during the eighteenth century," and sees it as a "product of man's preoccupation with a rational universe, an emphasis on the eternal force of religious emotion on man's soul, and the longing to define man's place in nature."[292] Such an ambiguity of religion and science is quite apparent in the *Essay*. On the one hand Clarkson offers scientific explanations for man's diversity but on the other hand, he seems to feel the need to supply a Scriptural illustration as well.

In *Complexion of Race*, Roxann Wheeler points out that towards the end of the eighteenth century a paradigm shift in ideas about the differences between people occurred. While up to that period mainly culture had served as distinction

---

[291] cf. Clarkson, *Essay* 74 (Part 3, chap. VIII).

[292] Mosse, *Eighteenth-Century Foundations* 41.

marker, it was then that the interest shifted to physical or bodily markers.[293] Both elements can be found in Clarkson's writings. She also points to the paradoxical fact that "the anti-slave trade position relied more heavily on appeals to racial similarity than slavery advocates relied on appeals to racial difference."[294] Peter Kitson also comments on the over-emphasis of the race issue in abolitionist writings. He holds that the importance attributed to the discussion of racial issues, by writers like Ramsey and Clarkson, is not justified by the arguments of their opponents because "actual public racialist justifications of slavery and the slave trade in the period 1780-1815 were comparatively rare."[295] Regarding Clarkson's work in particular Kitson points out that in it we find Christian essentialism combined with contemporary scientific awareness. The main point about Clarkson's discussion of skin colour is that he seeks to minimize its importance and that he tries to argue against scientific racism by giving his own arguments a scientific underpinning. It is ironical therefore, that in the abolitionist writings ideas of "'scientific racism' are most apparent, albeit under pressure of refutation."[296]

Thus Clarkson's theory of difference in physiology, such as skin colour, as an adaptation to environment, has two main implications: It has to be remarked positively that it negates Western assumptions of superiority, by depicting white as just as far removed from the original colour of dark olive as black. On the other hand, however, Clarkson's line of thoughts also points to the fact that Africans are indeed better suited to endure hot climate and thus make better workers in such places.

#### *4.1.7 A Short Summary of the Remaining Chapters*

In the penultimate chapter of his essay Clarkson deals with some more arguments of the 'receivers' of the slaves. Here he deals with arguments that compare the "state of the slaves with that of some of the classes of free men, and in certain scenes of felicity, which the former are said to enjoy."[297] First he

---

[293] cf. Wheeler, *The Complexion of Race* 237.
[294] ibid.
[295] Kitson, *Candid Reflections* 11.
[296] cf. ibid. 21.
[297] Clarkson, *Essay* 78 (Part 3, chap. IX).

dismisses a comparison of slaves with soldiers as far as their punishments are concerned. In the case of the soldier there exists a military court, whereas the "unhappy African"[298] is punished purely at the discretion of his lord. The second comparison Clarkson declares as not being valid is evaluating the situation of the slave as happier than that of an English peasant. Clarkson's counter-argument is that, if this was true, all the fictitious writers who choose the cottage as a place of happiness in their work, and who envy the felicity of the peasant would be wrong.[299] This distinction between peasant and slave is an important one. By it England is defined as free soil.

He then refutes the planters' pseudo-idyllic version of the slaves' daily lives in which they have time to plant their own little spots of land and from time to time even hold their tribal dances. Again Clarkson unfolds a piece of fiction in front of us. In a little story a penitent plantation owner tells his slaves:

> 'Africans! I begin at last to feel for your situation; and my conscience is severely hurt, whenever I reflect that I have been reducing those to a state of misery and pain, who have never given me offence. [...] I will therefore make you a proposal. Will you be content to live in the colonies, and you shall have the half of every week entirely to yourselves? Or will you choose to return to your miserable, wretched country?'[300]

His offer induces the following response:"[…] 'Behold! they are now flying from the dance: you may see them running to the shore, and, frantick as it were with joy, demanding with open arms an instantaneous passage to their beloved native plains.'"[301]

This reaction of the slave is the very opposite of what Clarkson promises in his later work. In his *Thoughts* he suggests on almost every possible occasion that the slaves, after their emancipation, will obediently stay in their position as servants for the mutual benefit of both themselves and their masters. He concludes the *Essay* with a summary of his main arguments. Slavery is "contrary to *reason, justice, nature, the principles of law and government, the whole doctrine, in short, of natural religion, and the revealed voice of God.*"[302]

---

[298] ibid. 79 (Part 3, chap. IX)
[299] cf. ibid. 79 (Part 3, chap. IX).
[300] Clarkson, *Essay* 81 (Part 3, chap. IX).
[301] ibid.
[302] ibid. 90 (Part 3, chap. XI)

### *4.1.8 Ideological Parameters of the Essay*

I would like to summarize the ideological sources which Clarkson mainly draws on in his *Essay* briefly. I have shown that humanitarian arguments, in the form of sentimental rhetoric, are important for the text. Several sentimental strategies have been explained. Clarkson's humanitarianism is influenced by his ideas about 'natural law,' which provide him with a rational explanation as to why slavery is immoral. Of course also other parameters are important, such as the relevance of Clarkson's quite frequent references to the Bible which is part of the religious parameter of the *Essay*. I mentioned his literal use of the Bible as a historical source. Tradition as a justifier for the present conditions adds a historical dimension to arguments. This can be found especially at the beginning of the *Essay* where Clarkson explains the history of slavery. It is there that Clarkson depicts slavery as an atavism while not regarding European traditions of bound labour a form of slavery as one.

Clarkson also refutes slavery due to its illegitimacy according to concepts of natural law. In the part about the historical development of the social contract history and natural law are amalgamated. In this way Clarkson's depiction of history as an aimed and strictly logical process links it to the author's ideas about state reason and natural law. In this context the influence of Hobbes and Locke has been explained.

The last part of the *Essay* served me to illustrate Clarkson's concepts of race. I have explained that race is an important category for Clarkson, and how it is linked with religious essentialism. The concept of nation is strongly connected with his racial ideas in the *Essay*. It is primarily used in a contrastive way in terms of difference between 'civilized' and 'barbaric' nations. Although Clarkson tries to play down the influence of phenotypic difference on human's abilities, the fact still seems to worry him sufficiently to dedicate a quite substantial part of the Essay to its discussion.

Religion, since it influences Clarkson's concept of race, his humanitarianism and his sentimental rhetoric, is a dominant parameter in the *Essay*. James

Walvin also comments on this; he sees the origins of the British antislavery movement to lie "in a feeling of outraged religious sensibility."[303]

The absence of other ideologies is quite striking in this early work of Clarkson. Economic considerations, for example, do not play an important part in the *Essay*. The concept of nation is present but not used in national-economic terms. And also references to English law are practically non-existent. Clarkson deals with justice of a higher sort, by discussing religiously influenced concepts of natural law.

## *4.2* Clarkson's *Impolicy*

### *4.2.1 General Remarks Concerning Part I*

Clarkson's second work, *Impolicy*, is the outcome of his research in the main British slave ports and of his interviews with crew members. Concerning Clarkson's biography it has to be remarked that *Impolicy* is the first writing he produced as a member of the 'Society for the Abolition of the Slave Trade.' *Impolicy*, quite drastically, depicts the conditions of the crews of the slave ships. The aim of its first part is to show that the slave trade is far from beneficial to the British nation and to suggest that an alternative trade in African natural goods instead of slaves. The suffering of the British sailors and the economic disadvantages of the slave trade are the main concerns in this text.

Both Clarkson's later works, *Impolicy* and *Thoughts,* show much more concern with national-economic and political issues. This is quite significant since these are the pieces he wrote after his first direct contacts with the British abolition movement. It is therefore justified to suggest an influence of his political activities for the abolitionist society. Obviously Clarkson wrote his *Essay* from a less involved position than the two later texts.

This might also be the reason why historical interpretations of the antislavery movement's aims, such as Davis' or Drescher's, apply better to *Impolicy* and *Thoughts*. In Davis' terms these later essays reflect the "ideological needs of

303 James Walvin, "The Propaganda of Anti-Slavery," *Slavery and British Society: 1776-1846,* ed. James Walvin (Baton Rouge: Louisiana State University Press, 1982) 63.

various groups and classes"[304] more obviously. Through his involvement with abolitionist society Clarkson certainly had become part of an ideological group. Davis states that new ideological needs were created by such events as the French and Industrial Revolution and by an emerging nationalism.[305] The first two influence Clarkson's writings in terms of a bigger emphasis on issues of free labour and personal freedom, the latter shows in his discussion of slave trade in the context of competing European nations.

### *4.2.2 Economic Considerations*

Clarkson describes the African continent as abounding with commodities such as gums, wax, ambergris, honey, ivory, gold, woods, spices, drugs, dyes and even with "hidden treasures"[306] such as "have been hardly noticed"[307] by Europeans. Therefore, according to Clarkson, two possible lines of trade exist in Africa: natural goods such as wood or spices, and slaves. These two kinds of trade are constructed as being the exact opposite of each other and as mutually excluding each other. While slave trade is mainly connected with attributes of brutality, dirt, and sickness, the trade with natural goods is depicted as clean, healthy and beneficial.

The native Africans, who "are mostly in an unimproved state, and at best ignorant of the various mechanical arts that are practiced in Europe,"[308] do consequently not know about the valuable possessions they have. Clarkson sees the reason for their ignorance to be a by-product of the slave trade. This trade is depicted as hindering other commerce with Africa, by making the natives uncooperative and by wasting Britain's naval capacities.

Free labour and free enterprise, not slavery are the means to reap the incredible African riches. Clarkson points out that whenever the opportunity of such an additional trade in natural goods was offered to the natives, they "were no sooner made acquainted with, than embraced the plan [and] began to collect the

---

304 David Brion Davis, *The Problem of Slavery in the Age of Revolution, 1770-1823* (Ithaca: Cornell University Press, 1975) 42.

305 cf. ibid.

306 Clarkson, *Impolicy* 7.

307 ibid.

308 ibid. 8.

different articles accordingly."[309] Thus he makes two propositions: "First, that the Africans, by proper encouragement can be brought into habits of labour: and secondly that free labour can be made the medium through which the productions of their country may be collected [...]"[310] In connection with wood cutting he points out that "the exertions of free, compared with those of servile labour, are at least in the proportion of three to two."[311] Thus the wood "would be brought into the hands of the merchant and manufacturer, cheaper by more than a third than it comes to them at present."[312] I think the following paragraph tells a lot about the reformer Thomas Clarkson, and his free-labour credo:

> Indigo also is prejudicial to the health of those who manufacture it. This is occasioned by the offensiveness of the effluvia, which arise from it at that time. Now as these manufacturers are slaves, it is impossible that the proprietors of them can furnish it so cheap a rate, as those who would employ free men, and who, in the case of the death of their labourers, could renew them without expense.[313]

We have to ask, 'Where is the philanthropist now, the abolitionist saint?' Little of the earlier compassion for the 'unfortunate Africans' seems to be left. Although Clarkson remarks in the next paragraph, that also "a considerable portion of human life would be saved",[314] if free Africans were employed, because they have a way of preparing the article with but little detriment to their health, he mentions this only in the second place, and still seems to find the death of some Africans a necessary evil in exchange for Europe's supply with goods.

National and economic ideology interact and become more important in *Impolicy*. Clarkson tries to evaluate the national consequences of abolition. Arguments of British autarchy play an important role in these considerations. Regarding the country's supply with spices he states that "the Dutch supply us at present with these articles. They have become of late very exorbitant in their demands [...], as they have a monopoly in the trade." Consequently, "were our attention turned to the encouragement of these articles on the coast [of Africa], it is clear that we might be the importers of our own spices, and break the

---

309 ibid. 3.
310 ibid. 5.
311 ibid. 10.
312 ibid. 12.
313 ibid. 17.
314 ibid. 17.

monopoly of this trade."[315] He applies the same argument to the spices and drugs which are imported from South America. Ideas of competing European nations are quite dominant in the *Impolicy*. Later in the text, Clarkson also considers the high death rate among the sailors employed in the trade at quite some length in connection with the balance of naval strength among the European powers.

Considering the public advantages of an abolition of the slave trade, and the resulting enhanced trade in natural commodities, it appears to Clarkson that "they would afford an inexhaustible mine of wealth to our dyers and artificers in wood; that they would enable us to break the monopoly of the Dutch; would repay us for the loss of America; be the cheapest market for all sorts of raw materials for our manufacturers; and abound with other national advantages."[316] Clarkson shows that financial investments in the slave trade are also quite hazardous and unprofitable for the individuals involved. He even compares investments in the trade with participating in a lottery or other games of chance. Consequently he suggests, regarding the commerce in productions of the coast: "It is clear, in the first place, that this commerce would not be equally hazardous with the former; rice, indigo, tobacco, spices and other productions of Africa not being perishable commodities like slaves."[317] He uses three more arguments to explain why this sort of trade would be more advantageous. The first is that the merchants would receive their returns in only five months as opposed to three years in the triangle trade. The next is that insurance would be considerably less, by which five percent would be saved. The final result of direct trade with Africa would be that the ships could make two journeys during the time in which one Atlantic triangle is performed, thus again enhancing the profits.

Clarkson then, at quite some length, shows that the trade in African goods would not interfere with the trade with Britain's own colonies, because it would only make up for the amount of goods that are imported from the colonies of such "rival states" [318] as the Netherlands, France or Spain.

---

[315] ibid. 14.
[316] ibid. 22.
[317] ibid. 26.
[318] ibid. 30.

### *4.2.3 Ideological Differences*

So far, the moral and sentimental arguments that can be found in the *Essay* are almost completely absent in *Impolicy*. What Clarkson mainly relies on are the economic reasons for the impolicy of the trade. A reason for that surely is the data which he used for this essay.

As I have already mentioned in connection with the passage about the production of indigo, the "heartfelt outrage"[319] about the slavery as such is replaced by sometimes even cynical economic deliberations about production costs. The very avarice Clarkson holds responsible for slavery in the *Essay*,[320] becomes his argument against it in *Impolicy*. Another by-product of the economic approach to slavery is that the Africans are turned into a commodity.[321]

I think Clarkson's, by then professional, involvement in abolitionist society could be the cause for that. In this respect it is important to remember that in its meeting on 24th of March 1787 the London Committee chose to abolish the slave trade, and not slavery as such. Perhaps they felt that arguing on a purely idealistic and moral basis would not be as effective with their audiences as 'rational' arguments, or they might really have believed to be "laying the axe at the very root" [322] of the evil. Whatever the reason, it is a fact that the abolitionists' goal at this time was not to ensure emancipation for Africans. The outcome of this was that chattel slavery was simply replaced by forms of wage slavery.

Clarkson's free-labour ideology is similar to Adam Smith's in *Wealth of Nations,* in which he states that the "master"[323] does not have to pay for the "wear and tear"[324] of the free labourer, while he has to pay for that of the slave. Therefore, "the experience of all ages and nations [...] demonstrates that the work done by slaves, though it appears to cost only their maintenance, is in the

---

[319] Hochschild, *Bury the Chains* 91.

[320] cf. Clarkson, *Essay* 24 (part 2, chap. VII).

[321] cf. Clarkson, *Impolicy* 26.

[322] Clarkson, *History* 149 (chap. XIII).

[323] Adam Smith, *An Inquiry into the Nature and Causes of the Wealth of Nations.* (5. Sept. 2006 http://www.gutenberg.org/dirs/etext02/wltnt11.txt) chap. II.

[324] ibid.

end the dearest of any."[325] In the part of *Impolicy* dealing with indigo production one can see that Clarkson takes over Smith's point of view, in which not the suffering human provides the rationale against slavery but the employer's want for maximum profit. Although such arguments might seem economically correct, they are, however, certainly questionable from a moral point of view. The humane side of abolition is degraded to a by-product of profit maximizing.

### *4.2.4 National Dimension of the Trade*

To back up the rational and economic arguments, sentimental rhetoric is present again in the remaining chapters of the *Impolicy's* first part. Having considered the slave trade in an "abstracted light"[326] and having "balanced it both nationally and individually"[327] against the advantages of "one in the productions of the coast",[328] Clarkson now turn to the "appendages" of the trade, which are said to be "of the highest importance to the state".[329]

In chapters IV and V Clarkson refutes the argument that the slave trade is a nursery for seamen and provides them with work. He presents the data he collected concerning this by means of tables, which are supplemented by his rather explicit depiction of the incredible cruelties of the sailors' daily routine. The suffering of the African 'cargo,' however, is mostly excluded.

The first of the appendages he mentions is that the trade offers work to many sailors and provides a "nursery for our seamen."[330] To refute this argument of the 'patrons' of the trade, Clarkson first unfolds the "history of the seamen employed in this trade."[331] Under this header he informs us that, due to the difficulty to find seamen to serve aboard slave vessels, recruiting practices include false promises of promotion, making them drunk, and other sorts of cheating the sailors into signing a contract. Such customs, Clarkson states, are unique to the slave trade. Considering his extensive travelling and interviewing

325 ibid.
326 Clarkson, *Impolicy* 30.
327 ibid.
328 ibid.
329 ibid. 31.
330 ibid.
331 ibid.

of persons concerned, before the composition of *Impolicy*, Clarkson was obviously quite well informed on the topic. He points out that the sailors have to sign their dubious contracts hurriedly and without properly reading them. Clarkson contrasts this with the less crooked practices in the wood trade with the same African coast.

Concerning the treatment of sailors during the journey, instead of talking "in general terms of the cruelties exercised upon the seamen" he resolves to confine himself "for the present to the occurrences in one ship."[332] What follows can be regarded as a sentimental narrative again. Clarkson states his intent to include it in his line of arguments because otherwise he would "have but little attention paid to my narration by the public."[333] Taking the muster roll of one ship in the triangle trade, he shows the fate of the individuals on it. In order to arouse the readers' compassionate feelings Clarkson does not spare us with plenty of detail. Just a bit will serve as an example:

> [the surgeon's mate of the ship] was beaten up so unmercifully by the captain, as to be taken up insensible. The brute [i.e. the captain], not satisfied with this, pushed the stick of his umbrella against his belly as he was lying upon the ground. [...] On the sixteenth day of the next month [...] he immediately seized him, and knocked him down. He then jumped upon his breast. He afterwards beat him in a cruel manner with the but [sic!] end of the cat [...Other persons on the ship too were] knocked down without any just cause.[334]

Clarkson takes especial pain to describe the treatment of one African crew member by the sadist captain. The one African person aboard the ship has to stand in place of all the other suffering Africans. Not only does the 'brute' frequently chase his dog after him, but "so much pleasure did he receive from the exercise of cruelty and oppression, that he became the executioner on these occasions."[335] Still not enough:

> At another time he was flogged as before, and so severely, that he was cut from the neck to the small of the back in a shocking manner. When the operation was over, the captain called for a bucket, in which he mixed pepper and salt water, and then anointed his back, with a view to increase his pain. In short, so barbarous was his conduct to this poor fellow, that he became insensible at last, and, full of scars, and

[332] ibid. 36.
[333] ibid. 36.
[334] ibid. 40f.
[335] ibid. 42.

unable to walk upright, he frequently crawled in his chain, like a dog, upon all fours;[336]

In the next section of the chapter, sailors are branded with hot iron pokers and beaten up for so long, that three executioners tire and a 'cat' is worked up. Needless to say, that the victims of such excesses did not have any chance for redress.

In chapter V Clarkson presents tables containing statistic facts about numbers of casualties. He explains the death of sailors during the journeys is only one part of the national loss in seamen, caused by the slave trade. Some of the sailors, due to their cruel treatment, turn their back on seafaring at all, while others desert ship in the West Indies, where they either stay and die or return home maimed or infirm, and not of any use for society. Of course their different ways of death are again described in quite some detail.

Clarkson calculates this form of loss by comparing the crew numbers of the ships with the number on their death lists. The outcome of all his calculations taken together is that the slave trade loses more men in one year than all the other naval trades taken together in two. The obvious conclusion he draws is that the slave trade, far from being a nursery for seamen, rather is their grave.[337]

As I have shown, elements of sentimental rhetoric can again be identified in the above chapters. The persuasive aim Clarkson follows with these passages is to make the audiences feel sorry for the poor sailors in the trade. In Carey's terms, the sentimental narratives serve as an emotional subversion of the intellect, in that an emotional passage (i.e. the description of the cruel treatment of the sailors) precedes the rational argument (i.e. the calculations based on the crew lists) in order that the first enhances the effect of the latter.[338]

In sum, what Clarkson does again is to depict the slave trade as a non-progressive, anachronistic practise. His idea is that the despicable nature of the slave trade has a corrupting effect on all levels of the practice. By the description of the barbaric conditions under which the sailors have to work he tries to show how the character of the persons involved is corrupted. By means of such drastic descriptions, the slave trade is also contrasted to other naval

---

[336] ibid. 43.

[337] cf. ibid. 49.

[338] cf. Carey, *The Rhetoric of Sensibility* 42f.

trades, making it something essentially evil. Also Davis points out that most abolitionists took especial pains to accentuate the moral contrast between what they conceived of as the free and the slave worlds.[339]

### *4.2.5 Mortality of the Seamen and Alternatives*

In the next chapter therefore, Clarkson contrasts healthy and profitable trades like the wood trade to the disadvantageous slave trade. From an economic point of view he argues that these trades are much more profitable, because of shorter distances and shipping times. Furthermore, the new sort of trade could be conducted with the same ships and from the same coasts as the slave trade, only with less mortality. Here Clarkson tries to dispel the fears of the profiteers of the slave trade, his idea being that just as many ships would be used for the trade with natural goods as were used before for slave trade.[340]

Several causes for the high mortality rate aboard slave vessels are mentioned. Apart from the sailors' exposure to unhealthy climate on the coasts of Africa and further inland, when procuring the slaves in open boats, many are also lost to insurrections, and to contagious diseases spread by the Africans. Another reason for the high losses can be "found in that barbarous and oppressive treatment, which has been described".[341] Clarkson attributes the existence of this sort of treatment "to the nature of this execrable trade".[342] The unlimited power of the slave ship captains is in "general too much for the human mind to bear [...] The scenes too, which they must constantly be accustomed to behold, harden the heart, rob it of its finer feelings, and at length create a ferocity that, [...] renders them rather monsters than men."[343]

Other reasons for Clarkson are "bad living"[344] of the seamen, meaning that they are for the most part half starved, and do not get sufficient drink, which "greatly impoverishes their blood"[345] In addition to that they have to eat a lot of "salt

[339] cf. Davis, "Abolitionism and Ideological Hegemony" 165.
[340] cf. Clarkson, *Impolicy* 69-75.
[341] ibid. 69.
[342] ibid.
[343] ibid. 70.
[344] ibid.
[345] ibid.

provisions" [346] which "vitiate the juices",[347] cause scorbutic disorders, and "so thin their blood [that it] "discharged itself at the ulcerated places".[348] A last part of the unhealthy nature of the slave trade is that "when the slaves are brought on board, the seamen, to make room for them are turned out of their apartments between the decks,"[349] forcing them to sleep on the open deck during the middle passage. There they are exposed to the "inclemency of the weather,"[350] thus contracting further diseases such as fevers and rheumatisms, which render them "burthensome to themselves, and unserviceable to the state."[351]

The trade in natural African goods would be completely different. To begin with the sailors would not be exposed to the hostile African climate, since the merchandise, according to Clarkson's plan, would be brought to the trading posts on the coast. And probably even the climate itself would change due to the influence of increased civilization of the continent:

> [if] the forest were cleared, [...] the land were put in cultivation, [...] the swamps were drained, and such other events were to take place, as would be the certain effects of establishing the trade proposed, the causes of this mortality to strangers would gradually decrease, the dews would be moderated, the rains and tornadoes would become less frequent and violent, and the climate be as healthy as in any other region of the globe.[352]

And of course the fact that the slaves transmit diseases, does not apply to such a new kind of trade. In sum, the sailors would be able to perform their services on a healthy ship, which could be frequently supplied with fresh provisions from the coast.

The first part of *Impolicy* concludes with some more colonialist or even early imperialist considerations. The fact that British ships do not only bring slaves to British colonies, but also to French and Spanish, "enables them to clean an additional piece of ground" supplying an additional produce, employing "additional seamen; and the great number of naval subjects, which we thus additionally raise for an enemy, has a tendency [...] to diminish our naval

---

[346] ibid. 72.
[347] ibid.
[348] ibid.
[349] ibid. 71
[350] ibid.
[351] ibid.
[352] ibid. 69.

importance." [353] The diminishing effect of the trade on the British number of "naval subjects"[354] is of course fatal to the naval importance of the country. For Clarkson this is something which cannot be made up for by the positive sides of the trade.

### *4.2.6 Colonial Aspects*

The kind of thought we come across here has certain similarities to later, imperialist ideology. It is of course too early to speak of genuine imperialism in connection with Clarkson. Today it is generally acknowledged that a last big wave of Imperialism starts in the decades after 1870 and ends with the first world war.[355] In the British case the occupation of Egypt in 1882 is seen as the starting point of modern imperialism in Africa.[356] The underlying pattern of thought that the aim of foreign policy is to secure the biggest possible part of influence in the world for one's nation, however, can be observed in Clarkson's writings. As an alternative to slave trade, the establishment of trading posts in Africa becomes a moral obligation and justifies the exertion of influence. Davis argues that one of the abolitionists' aims was to export the ideology of wage labour throughout the world on moral grounds. This also served a domestic need to "valorise wage labour as a universal norm."[357] In times of the Industrial Revolution, and the introduction of new forms of exploitation and suffering, it was "by no means clear that the British working class was less victimized than were West Indian slaves",[358] or the sailors employed in slave trade in this case. Clarkson's antislavery texts are quite clear on this point. While slave trade is execrable, domestic forms of wage labour are used as the norm to measure the degree of inhumanity abroad. Even a cursory glance at British literature of the Victorian period suggests a less bright picture of domestic labour conditions.[359] Therefore, Clarkson's depiction of the incredible suffering that occurred in the

---

[353] ibid. 76/77.
[354] ibid. 76.
[355] cf. Gregor Schöllgen, *Das Zeitalter des Imperialismus,* Oldenburg Grundriss der Geschichte 15. (München: Oldenburg Verlag, 2000) 1.
[356] cf. ibid. 2.
[357] Davis, *Abolitionism and Ideological Hegemony* 165.
[358] ibid.
[359] For example Charles Dickens' or Elizabeth Gaskell's social problem novels.

slave trade, intentionally or not, led public attention away from domestic social issues.

Clarkson, as already mentioned, had no first hand information about Africa. In his description of the African continent his ignorance becomes quite evident. His image of Africa is mainly characterized by vast amounts of uncivilized land, and the extreme fecundity of the soil. A Sierra Leone Company to 'civilize' the country, founded within abolitionist circles and which proved a gigantic failure, can also be seen to have originated out of such a romantically transfigured view of Africa.[360] In Said's terms, what makes Clarkson's description of Africa an image is that a simplified picture represents or stands for a very large entity, otherwise impossibly diffuse, which it enables one to grasp or see.[361]

### *4.2.7 General Remarks Concerning Part II*

Having dedicated his deliberations in the first part to dispel arguments based on the alleged 'positive advantages' of slave trade, Clarkson's intention in the second part of his *Impolicy* is to refute such arguments in favour of slave trade as are drawn from the prediction of fatal consequences in the case of its abolition. In this part he mainly elaborates on demographic and economic predictions.

He bases his arguments on the assumption that if planters had to do without a continuous supply of fresh slaves from Africa, their self interest would bring them to treat their remaining slaves better, and even see to it, that their number might increase. It is important again to note here that Clarkson and his fellow abolitionists did not challenge the plantation system as such. In contrast to the passage in his *Essay*, in which the slaves jubilantly want to return home to Africa upon the news of their liberation,[362] his idea is now that they would obediently stay on the plantations, under a contract as paid labourers. Also Hochschild states that "Clarkson and his comrades were making clear that they opposed only slavery, not the plantation system itself."[363] Capitalist ideology manifests itself here: while it is immoral to keep someone under control by brute

[360] cf. Hochschild, *Bury the Chains* 177f.
[361] cf. Said, *Orientalism* 66.
[362] cf. Clarkson, *Essay* 81 (Part 3, chap. IX)
[363] Hochschild, *Bury the Chains* 324.

force, a more abstract form of control, via wage slavery, is perfectly acceptable. I have already stated in my discussion of *Impolicy's* first part that the aim was to transform the slaves into obedient and grateful labourers, working 'voluntarily' for wages. Davis states that the hope of achieving this aim rested on the assumption that the British system of wage labour "had achieved a reasonable balance between freedom and order and could serve as a norm against which harsher regimes could be measured."[364]

In his *Antislavery and Capitalism* Seymour Drescher holds that the process of abolition was closely embedded in the social and economic "context of a rising industrial order",[365] without which no such leverage for the transference of one form of social domination to another would have been available.[366] I think it is justified to see the antislavery movement in the context of the hegemonic process of the free labour ideology. Clarkson in particular focused "more on the corruption of the free market, in metropolitan terms, [than on] the mere existence of forced labour in the colonies."[367]

### *4.2.8 The West Indian Plantation System*

In the second part of Impolicy Clarkson tries to come up with an explanation why the planters in the Caribbean are not able to keep their slave populations stable and thus depend on a constant supply with new workers from Africa. If the slaves were treated well and cared for when they were sick, he asks, "what should hinder the Africans, peculiarly prolifick in their nature, carried to a climate similar to that which they have left, and treated with common humanity, from continuing their own species, and precluding the necessity of a supply?"[368] Before dealing further with the positive effects of a possible abolition of the trade, Clarkson inquires into the causes of the problematic demographic situation of the slave population in the Caribbean. He finds a first cause in the reasoning of many planters that it is more profitable for them to "work out a slave, by an uncommon imposition of labour, in five or six years, and supply his

---

[364] Davis, "Abolitionism and Ideological Hegemony" 165.

[365] Drescher, *Anti-slavery and Capitalism* 162.

[366] cf. ibid.

[367] ibid. 163.

[368] Clarkson, *Impolicy* 88.

place by a new recruit from the coast [...]". Were the supply cut off, this "diabolical determination" would stop, forcing the planters to "breed [sic!]" [369] their slaves, as Clarkson points out.
A second cause for the precarious demographic situation is the bad care that is taken of the slaves' children, who are left in the fields by their overworked parents, "exposed to a vertical sun, and afterwards to the dews of the evening [...]." [370] Again Clarkson points out that without a constant influx of new slaves, every possible attention would be given to the rearing of the new generations. He even suggests incentives to mothers, such as "a release from all future obligation to labour, after she had reared her third child "or by giving them a reward.[371]
The other causes are the "very scanty allowances of provision", "the incessant and intolerable labour", and finally the "cruel and severe usage".[372] These would all be done away with by the increased value of the slaves after abolition. And again Clarkson concludes that it is evident that the Africans would "continue their own species" and even, "being endued with a more prolifick nature than the rest, they must rapidly increase." So much so that the planters would soon be able "to put new land into cultivation without any purchase from the coast."[373]
Then further positive effects of abolition are shown. The planters would not need to spend money on slaves anymore, which Clarkson thinks to be the number one source for debts in the colonies. Additionally, their present fortune would rise because the slaves would become more valuable. Clarkson then pays particular attention to the fact that the workers of the future would not be native Africans anymore, who, "having led a life of indolence in their own country, have been but little capable of sustaining the fatigue which they have been sentenced to undergo."[374] The new generation of Creoles would learn the language and be used to doing plantation work from childhood on, thus the work would be done better and faster. Less insurrections would occur because, as

---

[369] ibid. 90.
[370] ibid. 92.
[371] ibid.
[372] ibid. 92/93.
[373] ibid. 94.
[374] ibid. 96/97.

Clarkson quite cynically remarks, "they would not be so keenly sensible of the loss of liberty, which is perhaps, of all others, the greatest incitement to an insurrection. A bird, that has been bred up in captivity, does not repine like one, that has been taken from the woods, and confined within the narrow limits of a cage."[375]

In this new, saver situation the planter would then be "smiling with gratitude and joy", and not be a "tyrant and destroyer [anymore], but the shepherd and guardian of his slaves."[376] Such a "golden age"[377] would have the advantage that the Creoles would become "steady and faithful protectors"[378] of the islands, thus freeing troops for other pursuits.

Such passages suggest a logical connection of capitalism and abolition. It can be established as a fact that Clarkson's and the abolitionists' main concern cannot have been a true emancipation, but merely to substitute capitalist methods of controlling a workforce for the violently forceful methods of feudal times. Clarkson obviously tries to appeal to the plantation owners in this passage. He never actually speaks to the slaves in person. In general Clarkson's texts are exclusively aimed at a European audience.

The replacement of one method of domination by another is what Seymour Drescher refers to as "the mighty experiment"[379] in his book of the same title. He argues that the progress of exchanging one sort of control with another is linked with the classic enlightenment paradigm, explaining the concept of human progress with "a shift from medieval servitude to modern, free, contractual bargaining."[380] This implied economic superiority of free over servile labour which "was essential for Western expansion and development".[381] Accordingly the works of Adam Smith became an important source of scientific

---

375 ibid. 99.

376 ibid. 102.

377 ibid.

378 ibid.

379 Drescher, *Mighty Experiment* 7.

380 ibid. 5.

381 ibid.

authority.[382] The importance of his ideology becomes quite evident in this second part of Clarkson's *Impolicy.*

### *4.2.9 National Aspects of Abolition*

Clarkson finally turns to the consequences of abolition for the British kingdom. First he dispels doubts about the loss of the revenues from the export of goods to Africa, by, rather expectedly, arguing that even more revenue could be gained from the sort of trade he advocates in the first part of *Impolicy.* In the West Indian colonies, "in what ever point of view we consider the subject, [...] it is highly probable that the revenue would be increased."[383]

Clarkson again predicts a rise in the slave populations, since "it is founded on the invariable rule of nature, on the immutable decrees of Deity, that every society of people, among whom the sexes are properly proportioned [...] must increase."[384] Again he shows his fascination with the fertility of Africans when he points out that they have advantages of a prolific nature and of living in a climate to which they have been habituated from infancy.[385] Be that as it may, so much would the population increase that Clarkson feels compelled to start calculating how much land is actually left. He points out that in Jamaica alone there would be about 2.350.000 acres of land still to be cultivated. Together with the more efficient cultivation of the existing land, the increase in production would be enormous.[386]

But also African colonisation such as "encouraging the infant settlements in Sierra Leon",[387] would bring a considerable gain for the British state. The cultivation of African soil "would shew an example to the natives."[388] Without the impediment of slave trade the civilization of the Africans would be promoted by the new trade. He describes the advantage for Britain like this:

> It would soften and polish their manners, and would bring them to a state of refinement, though not immediately great in itself, yet great in comparison of their

[382] cf. ibid. 7.
[383] Clarkson, *Impolicy* 108.
[384] ibid. 109.
[385] cf. ibid. 109.
[386] cf. ibid. 110
[387] ibid. 114.
[388] ibid.

former state. This civilization would be productive of the most beneficial effects to ourselves: for in proportion as we civilize a people, we increase their wants, and we should create therefore, from this circumstance alone, another source of additional consumption of our manufactures, even within the same space.[389]

This kind of thought was of course especially welcomed by northern English manufacturing towns, which would be able to sell their products to new settlements. It is at them that Clarkson's argument is obviously aimed.

He again concludes with a summarizing paragraph which runs: "whatever arguments the moralist is able to collect from the light of reason, or the man of humanity from his feelings, the statesman is able to collect others from the source of policy, that call equally aloud for its ABOLITION [sic!]."[390]

*4.2.10 Ideological Parameters of Impolicy*

I have shown, that the 'politick' arguments prevail in *Impolicy*. Obviously the moralist, humanitarian, and religious arguments are pushed aside by what Clarkson calls "policy".[391] Probably his greater involvement in politics due to his professional occupation as an antislavery lobbyist, led him to the conviction that arguing on a purely humane and moral basis might not be sufficient to persuade the interested parties of abolitionist aims.

In terms of ideological parameters, *Impolicy* shows a tendency away from religiously motivated arguments to a more rational refutation of the slave trade. Clarkson mainly argues against it by pointing to economic disadvantages. Now he also uses the concept of nation in a different way. His main national concern is to ensure the greatest possible economic benefit and global influence for the British nation. The national and the economic parameters are of course again supported by sentimental rhetoric. With vivid descriptions of the suffering of slaves and sailors Clarkson tries to rally the readers emotions against the trade.

Racial considerations can be found again in *Impolicy*. The concept of race serves Clarkson to establish differences between Europeans and Africans, especially that Africans are more proliferate and that they are better adapted to working in hot climate. I have already pointed out in my discussion of the racial parameter of the *Essay*, that such differentiating is a racist element of Clarkson's work.

[389] ibid. 115.
[390] ibid. 134.
[391] ibid.

In *Impolicy* Clarkson wants to raise awareness of the precariousness of the present situation of slaves and sailors; therefore, no such historical arguments as in the *Essay* can be found. Furthermore, there is strikingly less emphasis on the legal dimension of the trade, both in terms of natural and specific law.

One question which all scholars seem to have about abolitionism is why it was so successful. The different ways of answering it seem to have one similar direction. Most scholars, in Eric William's tradition, analyse the connection of abolitionist arguments with the ideological needs of interested classes. I hope to have made clear that Clarkson's arguments in *Impolicy* are quite consistent with this theory. Once a part of the abolitionist network, many of the reasons he brings forward against the slave trade are designed in a way to strike a chord with the emerging elite of the Industrial Revolution.

You cannot call Clarkson anything else but a cynic considering some of the passages cited above. His way of comparing the workers in the West Indies with caged birds is especially telling.[392] It gives evidence to Davis's[393] and Hochschild's[394] statements that the aim of abolitionism was not to liberate the slaves, but rather to educate and civilize Africans to become happy and content workers to ensure the continuation of the plantation system in the Caribbean and to justify further European involvement in Africa. Clarkson, quite openly, uses the very same avarice questioned on moral grounds in his *Essay,* to legitimate a new form of wage slavery in his *Impolicy*. This is a trend which becomes still more apparent in the next work of my discussion.

One thing we have to bear in mind is that, in *Impolicy,* Clarkson still believes simply abolishing the trade to be the best way to enhance the slaves' living conditions. To a certain extent, this changes in the next text.

---

[392] cf. ibid. 99.

[393] cf. David Brion Davis, "Slavery and 'Progress,'" *Anti-Slavery, Religion, and Reform: Essays in Memory of Roger Anstey,* eds. Chritine Bolt and Seymour Drescher (Folkestone, Kent, and Hamden, Connecticut: Dawson and Archon, 1980) 363.

[394] cf. Hochschild, *Bury the Chains* 324.

## 4.3 Clarkson's *Thoughts*

### *4.3.1 General Remarks*

In *Thoughts* Clarkson laments that the condition of the slaves in the colonies did not improve as much, as he predicted it would after the abolition of the trade. The main thing he wants to communicate to his readers is that emancipating the plantation slaves in a gradual way, would benefit both plantation owners and slaves. A huge part of the text consists of Clarkson's attempts to dispel anxieties about the conduct of the Caribbean slave populations after emancipation. In order to do this he lists several recent historical examples of emancipations of groups of slaves to show that social order was preserved after such an act.

An interesting thing can be observed in Clarkson's use of vocabulary: while he mainly talks about the "unfortunate", "wretched", or "unhappy" African in his *Essay*[395] he now refers to them mostly as "Negroes."[396] His use of sentimental attributes clearly declined. In the *Essay*, for example, one of his favourite adjectives to describe the Africans is "unfortunate,"[397] in *Thoughts* he does not use it even once. This simple linguistic fact can be seen as a further indicator for a change in his argumentative strategies from a more sentimental to a rather more rationally and economically based one.

### *4.3.2 Aim and Motivation of Thoughts*

The full title of this essay, *Thoughts On The Necessity Of Improving The Condition Of The Slaves In The British Colonies With A View To Their Ultimate Emancipation; And On The Practicability, The Safety, And The Advantages Of The Latter Measure* is quite symptomatic for Clarkson's creed. Even in the title he does not demand emancipation, but only offers his thoughts with "a view"[398]

---

[395] Query for keywords with AntConc in Clarkson's *Essay* (1.11.2006, http://www.gutenberg.org/files/10611/10611-h/10611-h.htm): 'unfortunate' used 42x, 'wretched' used 27x, 'unhappy' used 11x, referring to slaves, Africans etc.

[396] Query for keywords with AntConc in *Thoughts* (1.11.2006, http://www.gutenberg.org/files/10386/10386-h/10386-h.htm): 'unfortunate' used 0x, 'wretched' used 3x, 'unhappy' used 0x in referring to slaves, Africans etc.

[397] used 43x.

[398] Thomas Clarkson, "Thoughts on the Necessity of Improving the Condition of the Slaves in the British Colonies, With a View to their Ultimate Emancipation; and on the Practicability,

to final emancipation of the slaves, implying a process of education. Also in the preface to *Thoughts* Clarkson makes it once again quite clear, that the emancipation he desires "is such an Emancipation only, as I firmly believe to be compatible not only with the due subordination and happiness of the labourer, but with the permanent interests of his employer."[399]

Hochschild writes that a new group of abolitionists was formed in 1823 under the rather timid name 'London Society for Mitigating and Gradually Abolishing the State of Slavery Throughout the British Dominions.'[400] It is for this group that Clarkson composed *Thoughts*. He writes that the aims of this new society were "to civilize them [i.e. the slaves], to Christianise them... to make them better servants to their masters, and to make them more useful members of the community."[401] This shows that also this group of abolitionists did not dare to oppose the plantation system as such.[402]

In *Thoughts* Clarkson explains the abolitionists' original decision not to fight the institution of slavery as such but rather to attempt to abolish the trade again. He states that this was not because slavery was less wicked, but because there "were at the time not so many obstacles in the way of abolition, as of the Emancipation of the Negroes."[403] He explains that three effects were expected of this step. Firstly, the masters would have to take better care of their slaves and eventually the colonial laws would be changed accordingly. Secondly, allowing the slaves more freedom would make them better workers, which would, thirdly, "lead both masters and legislators on the score of interest to treat their slaves still more like men [...] till at length it would be no difficult task, and no mighty transition, to pass them to [...] the rank of free men."[404]

---

the Safety, and the Advantages of the Latter Measure," *Slavery, Abolition, and Emancipation: Writings in the British Romantic Period- Vol. 3 The Emancipation Debate*, ed. Debbie Lee (London: Pickering and Chatto, 1999) 82.

399 ibid. 83.

400 cf. Hochschild, *Bury the Chains* 323.

401 Hochschild, *Bury the Chains* 323f.

402 cf. ibid. 324.

403 Clarkson, *Thoughts* 85.

404 ibid. 86.

Clarkson points out, regarding the effects of abolition so far, that it led to "a somewhat better individual treatment of the slaves than before",[405] the other two effects (i.e. more freedom and finally emancipation), however, are still to be waited for. He tries to show that the laws that were passed in favour of the plantation slaves were up to then ineffectual, and therefore calls for a new code of laws "more akin to the principle of reward than of punishment, privilege than of privation, and which shall have a tendency to raise or elevate their condition, so as to fit them by degrees to sustain the rank of free men."[406]
Clarkson then repeats the refutation of the concept of slavery as such. Here we find the same arguments based on principles of natural law which were already developed in the *Essay*. To this he adds an explanation that the children of slaves certainly do not belong to the owner of their parents. On the one hand, the owners of the parents do not have a just claim to them in the first place because they obtained them only by "fraud and violence"[407] and on the other, "they can surely have no right to the infant, who is born of a woman slave. If there be any right to it by nature, such right must belong not to the master of the mother, but to the mother herself."[408] Above all: "Every man who is born into the world, whether he be white or whether he be black, is born, according to Christian notions, a free agent and an accountable creature."[409]
From these religiously and morally motivated considerations Clarkson then turns to the practical side of emancipation. He states that it is the task of the British Parliament to revise the colonial legislation so that it is not repugnant to the laws of the home country.[410] According to these laws, he points out no slave owner in the colonies has a just title over a person, who "becomes free by English law the moment he reaches the English shore".[411] This is the first time Clarkson deals with specific legal actions and implications of emancipation.

---

[405] ibid.
[406] ibid. 90.
[407] ibid. 93.
[408] ibid. 94.
[409] ibid. 94.
[410] cf. ibid. 96.
[411] ibid. 99.

### 4.3.3 Examples of Previous Emancipation

Another new element in the *Thoughts* is Clarkson's concern with the safety of the Emancipation of "a whole body of men".[412] Citing a Mr. W. Smith, MP for Norwich, Clarkson points out that "immediate emancipation might be an injury, and not a blessing to the slaves themselves"[413] and suggests the necessity of a period of preparation.

In *Thoughts* Clarkson again resorts to history for guidance, but as there "is no light from antiquity to guide on our way" to inquire into the effects of emancipating greater numbers of slaves at a time, he uses "six or seven instances of the emancipation of slaves in bodies"[414] during the last forty years, as examples.

The first four cases used in *Thoughts* are about Africans who had served in the British Army in the War of Independence and in the West Indies. Clarkson acknowledges that these cases are not exactly analogous to the West Indian slaves who "have been constantly in an abject and degraded state. Their faculties are benumbed. They have contracted all the vices of slavery. They are become habitually thieves and liars."[415] Again he states that such persons are not fit to receive their freedom. The slaves in his examples on the other hand, "found in the British army a school, as it were, which fitted them by degrees for making a good use of their liberty."[416] This sort of preparation is what Clarkson also recommends for the slaves in the sugar colonies. He adds that the fact that all the former slaves in his examples remained peaceful although experienced in the use of arms, is a positive indicator for the practicability and safety of emancipation on a larger scale.[417] The examples "afford us again ground for believing, that there is a peculiar softness, and plasticity, and pliability in the African character".[418] Clarkson contrasts the African character with the

412 ibid. 100.
413 ibid. 99.
414 ibid. 100.
415 ibid. 103.
416 ibid. 103.
417 cf. ibid. 103f.
418 ibid. 105.

"unbending ferocity of the North American Indians".[419] Finally Clarkson asks why the freed slaves should cut the throats of those who liberated them.

The fifth example are slaves of St. Domingo who were freed in the course of the French Revolution. Again Clarkson takes pains to prove that the freed slaves both remained peaceful and even resumed doing their work and obeying their masters. A first system of contractual labour was introduced by the two commissioners Polverel and Santhonax. It stated that "the labourers were obliged to hire themselves to their masters for not less than a year, at the end of which (September), but not before, they might quit their service, [...] and that they were to receive a third part of the produce of the estate, as a recompense for their labour."[420]

After that he describes that the African Toussaint-Louverture introduced an even more oppressive system of 'free' labour, in that he made the plantation workers "though free workers, a sort of adscripti glebae for five years."[421] Furthermore, he reduced the workers wages to one forth but "in the case only that the labourer clothed and maintained himself: where he did not do this, he was entitled to a fourth only nominally, for out of this his master was to make a deduction for board and clothing."[422]

Clarkson does not criticise this sort of keeping a workforce under strict dependence in the least, all he has to remark upon the code of Toussaint is that it "had the surprising effect of preserving tranquillity and order and of keeping up a spirit of industry on the plantations of St. Domingo."[423] It is obvious that in Clarkson's opinion the West Indian workforces need a strong hand in the transition phase to emancipation. This shows again that labour discipline, rather than freedom, is the thing that Clarkson is really concerned about.

As a sixth example he briefly mentions those slaves "who began to be liberated about eighteen months ago in the newly erected State of Columbia"[424] by

---

[419] ibid.
[420] ibid. 114.
[421] ibid. 115.
[422] ibid. 115.
[423] ibid.
[424] ibid. 117.

General Bolivar. In this case Clarkson points out that there only those with the best character were enfranchised.

### *4.3.4 Joshua Steele's Experiment*

The last example of an emancipation Clarkson uses is the experiment by Joshua Steele, "whose emancipation was attempted in Barbadoes [sic!] between 1783 and 1790."[425] This is the case Clarkson reports about in most detail. It serves him as a model case. Clarkson's source for his account of Steele's experiment is William Dickson's work *Mitigation of Slavery: Letters and Papers of the Late Honourable Joshua Steele.*

He shows how, in 1780, Mr. Steele resolved to run his estate personally to make it more profitable for himself and less destructive for its workforce. Disagreeing strongly with the present management of the workers he resolved to make experiments gradually on his estate to find answers to three questions:

> 1. Whether he could not do away all arbitrary punishments and yet keep up discipline among the slaves? 2. Whether he could not carry on the plantation-work through the stimulus of reward? 3. Whether he could not change slavery into a condition of a milder name and character, so that the slaves should be led by degrees to the threshold of liberty, from whence they might step next, without hazard, into the rank of free men, if circumstances should permit and encourage such a procedure.[426]

Steele's experiment included the introduction of a "magistracy out of the Negroes"[427] and a system of reward instead of punishment. Steele's introduction of a Negro-court is described to be quite ingenious for two reasons. Firstly because "it may be always at hand", and secondly because it "would give consequence to those Negroes who should compose it [...]; and everything, that might elevate the Black character, would be useful to those on the road to emancipation."[428]

Steele divided his land into manors, lordships and precincts and registered all adult male slaves as "copyholders."[429] Clarkson states that Mr. Steele "took the hint for the particular mode of improving the condition of his slaves [...] from

---

[425] ibid. 118.
[426] ibid. 119.
[427] ibid. 120.
[428] ibid. 124.
[429] ibid. 122.

the practice of our Anglo-Saxon ancestors in the days of Villainage."[430] Steele gave to his slaves "separate tenements of lands, which they were to occupy, and upon which they were to raise whatever they might think most advantageous to their support."[431] These tenements could be inherited by their children, thus attaching the Negroes to the soil. As a rent the copyholders had to work for 260 days a year for their master.

The connection with the Anglo-Saxon heritage in abolitionist discourse is by no means accidental. The author takes care not to depict the feudal system as a form of slavery. Clarkson, or the source from which he quotes, quite intentionally contrasts the situation of the slave with the one of the allegedly happy English peasants of earlier times. This is a technique which probably worked best in those areas of England that were most affected by the rapid industrialisation of the early 19th century. Romantic images of a pre-industrial society are used to arouse positively nostalgic feelings of a society in a process of rapid urbanization and industrialisation.[432]

Clarkson points out that the result of Steele's experiment was "highly satisfactory to himself".[433] And that both of the last mentioned cases certainly led to an improvement of their moral character and to their acquiring a spirit of industry. All the mentioned examples serve Clarkson to show that emancipation "is not only practicable, but that it is practicable without danger".[434] The possible danger for Clarkson are insurgencies and the deterioration of labour discipline. Consequently he tries to calm such anxieties by stating that in all his six examples the freed slaves were found to be "*yielding themselves to the will of their superiors*, so as to be brought by them *with as much ease and certainty into the form intended for them*, as clay in the hands of the potter is fashioned to his own model." Furthermore, he attests that "the Negro character is malleable at the European will."[435]

---

[430] ibid. 121.
[431] ibid. 122.
[432] cf. Drescher, *Anti-slavery and Capitalism* 163.
[433] Clarkson, *Thoughts* 123.
[434] ibid. 126.
[435] ibid.

In the subsequent part of *Thoughts* the positive effects of Steele's experiment are explained. Citing Adam Smith's famous dictum that free labour is much cheaper than slave labour he sets out to show the incredible increases in profit that were made on this sample plantation. Drawing on a Henry Botham's evidence he then compares the sugar industry of East India to the one of the West Indies, concluding that "sugar, better and cheaper than in the West Indian Islands, was produced by free men."[436] Clarkson then shows that the hope of personal gain is the stimulus which "gives birth to industry in any part of the world, seeing that work is not agreeable to man [...]"[437] As evidence to this he asks the question of why the English labourer does work more in a day than a slave. The answer is, of course, "the knowledge, that what he earns is for himself and not for another."[438]

In his conclusion Clarkson again makes a connection with East India and the East India Company: "They, the East India Company, again, have been a blessing to the Natives with whom they have been concerned. They distribute an equal system of law and justice to all without respect of persons. They dispel the clouds of ignorance, superstition, and idolatry, and carry with them civilization and liberty wherever they go."[439] The connection to imperial ventures of later decades is an obvious one.

The logical conclusion to establish a similar system in the West Indian Islands is not very far fetched. Advocating such a system had of course far reaching consequences on the future development of British policies in the colonies. In the final remark of his *Thoughts* Clarkson tries to form a bridge between ethical and rational considerations, saying that the "ways of unrighteousness are not profitable."[440]

---

[436] ibid. 132.
[437] ibid. 134.
[438] ibid.
[439] ibid. 144.
[440] cf. ibid.

*4.3.5 Freedom or Labour Discipline*

The fact that he does not develop any critique concerning Steele's experiment allows us to judge that for Clarkson it serves as an ideal type to illustrate his own vision of the future social order in the West Indian sugar colonies.

Seymour Drescher, however, does not speak in such favourable terms of Steele's experiment calling it "a modest experiment in quasi emancipation".[441] While he acknowledges that Steele's estate had a short time of prosperity in the 1780s, he states that by 1823 the experiment had become rather an embarrassment. He sees the initial run down state of the plantation as being one of the reasons for the initial success of the new way of management. Another would be the generally favourable economic situation of the sugar industry in the late 1780s and early 1790s. Drescher states that after 1783 the plantation did not continue to be successful at all and was finally sold for debt. He furthermore points out that for the abolitionists this failure seemed to be irrelevant, since they directed their interests more in the direction of the sources of the success of this experiment than in that of the causes of its failure.[442] This is quite apparent in *Thoughts*. Although written in 1823 we find not a single word about any negative aspects.

Another interesting aspect of *Thoughts* is the comparison of Steele's organisation of the estate with an Anglo Saxon model. The ancient English system of husbandry is depicted as an alternative to the cruel methods which prevailed in West Indian slavery. David Brion Davis states that the contrasting of the two is by no means accidental, but served the hegemonic function to define Britain as free soil. Thus the African slave's working conditions defined, by negative polarization, the means of coercion that were acceptable and which not.[443] He writes: "[…] antislavery provided a bridge between pre-industrial and industrial values; by combining the ideal of emancipation with an insistence on duty and subordination."[444]

[441] Drescher, *Mighty Experiment* 111f.

[442] cf. ibid.

[443] cf. Davis, *Abolitionism and Ideological Hegemony* 168f.

[444] cf. Davis, *Abolitionism and Ideological Hegemony* 170.

Davis refers to abolitionism as the rising British middle classes' way of constructing a free England in contrast to an unfree Africa and unfree colonies. He argues that "the slave owner's claims contrasted sharply with those of the idealized British squire, whose authority was constrained by law and custom, and with the rights of the rising capitalist, who was content to purchase labour in the market like any other commodity".[445] Contrasting the British system of wage labour to African slavery offered "both national and local ruling elites an increasingly attractive opportunity to demonstrate their commitment to decency and justice."[446] However, Davis wants to suggest a more complex model of abolitionism, than simply that of a screening device to attract attention away from metropolitan exploitation. From him the antislavery movement "mirrored the needs and tensions of a society increasingly absorbed with problems of labour discipline [...]."[447] The assumption of the superiority of wage-labour over slave labour, and Clarkson's concern about labour discipline, can be found in most of the arguments in *Thoughts*.

Davis also points out that "even Thomas Clarkson, who retained much of the liberal spirit of the late 1780s and 1790s, found nothing inequitable about coerced labour. Any state, he said, could legitimately use convicts to work in mines or clear rivers. What outraged Clarkson and other abolitionists was the claim of personal proprietorship that justified arbitrary and unlimited authority."[448]

From any of Clarkson's works, it is in *Thoughts* that a connection between a capitalist free labour ideology and the cause of abolitionism, or even emancipation in this case, is most apparent. Attempting to connect these two sets of values places Clarkson in a dilemma, trying to advocate emancipation and sustaining labour discipline, both at a time. Hochschild's statement that the abolitionists opposed slavery but not the plantation system is also confirmed by what Clarkson writes. Sometimes it almost appears as if he did not argue in favour of the oppressed Africans anymore, but rather for plantation owners, by

[445] Davis, *Abolitionism and Ideological Hegemony* 171.
[446] ibid. 170.
[447] ibid. 168.
[448] ibid. 171.

promising them enormous increases in their profits.[449] Which is probably even true, since Clarkson does address the oppressed Africans but tries to persuade their masters of the advantages of emancipation.

### *4.3.6 Ideological Parameters of Thoughts*

With its concern about issues of labour discipline *Thoughts* again shows an emphasis on economic issues. In contrast to *Impolicy* the concept of nation is again rather used in a contrastive way and not so much in imperialist terms. Concepts like nation and race are amalgamated in the parts dealing with the 'African character'.

In order to show the practicability of emancipation Clarkson uses recent historical events to point out the safety of such a step. I mentioned several examples of that. I also pointed out how in connection with Joshua Steele's experiment the history of the English feudal system is used to hint at nostalgic stereotypes and thus utilizes the later to define England as free soil.

*Thoughts* is the only one of Clarkson's essays that contains a discussion of the specific legal steps that have to be taken in order to emancipate the West Indian slave populations. Clarkson suggests that the colonies send in their constitutions in order to have them revised by British Parliament. At the beginning of *Thoughts* references to natural law and religion can be found again. They, however, are only a repetition of such arguments which are already found in the *Essay*. The main part of *Thoughts* rather deals with issues of safety and labour discipline.

I have pointed out already at the beginning of my discussion of *Thoughts* that there is less use of sentimental rhetoric than in the *Essay* and in *Impolicy*. Only in the repetitive part in the beginning of the text does Clarkson deal with the humanitarian side of emancipation. In all the other parts of *Thoughts* the main arguments for emancipation are safety and economic benefits for the plantation owners.

---

[449] cf. Hochschild, *Bury the Chains* 324.

## 5 Conclusion

With the help of the ideological parameters 'economy', 'history', 'humanitarianism', 'specific law', 'natural law', 'nation', 'race', and 'religion' I have tried to analyse Clarkson's basic assumptions and convictions concerning these ideologies.

In my examination of Clarkson's main lines of thoughts, I have identified the influence of colonial interest and elements of racism in his writings. With Carey's ideas of sentimental rhetoric I tried to get a deeper insight into Clarkson's way of presenting his arguments by tapping his readers emotions. These elements have, of course, to be seen in a larger context. I have shown how both Clarkson's lingering racism, his sentimental persuasion, and the colonial aspects of his writings are put in the service of his large scale abolitionist aims. Clarkson's aims were, of course, not static, but subject to change. In his *Essay* he still very much attacks the concept of slavery as such on religious and humanitarian grounds, but also with arguments based on concepts of natural law. The main concern of *Impolicy* is to depict the transatlantic trade as counter to national interest. Although Clarkson repeats his original concern of human bondage in the beginning of *Thoughts,* the main emphasis of the rest of this work is on the plantation owners' economic concerns and on the safety aspect of emancipation.

I think it has become apparent by now how Clarkson's style and arguments changed from 1787 to 1823. While the religious, the humanitarian and the natural-law parameters forms the basis in his early work the *Essay*, his two later pieces *Impolicy* and *Thoughts* show increasingly more concern with economic and national considerations. For example, Clarkson increasingly emphasizes the benefits of an emancipation for the West Indian plantation owners in economic terms. I have also pointed out that *Thoughts* is the only text which contains a discussion of English law. In the other texts he mainly relies on philosophical arguments.

Both in *Thoughts* and in the *Essay* Clarkson uses history in order to back up his statements. He depicts slavery as a gross antagonism in the *Essay,* and proves that emancipation is neither contrary to the interests of the planters nor dangerous in *Thoughts*. It is there that he also draws on Anglo-Saxon heritage to suggest a system of husbandry for the sugar colonies.

I have tried to connect Clarkson's work with more general historical interpretations of abolitionism, such as Davis' or Drescher's. These interpretations all suggest a strong connection between other interests and the moral claims of the abolitionists. Davis argues that concern with slavery abroad directed attention away from domestic problems of labour discipline. The question that had to be asked was why the abolitionist movement was so successful after all. I have shown that the reasons for the success of the antislavery movement can probably be found in the historical context of the time. It is important to note that Clarkson lived at the time of the French and Industrial Revolution. I pointed out how anti-slavery satisfied the ideological needs of rising capitalist elites and became part of an emerging imperialism.

**Bibliography**

Primary Texts:

Benezet, Anthony. *Some Historical Account of Guinea, Its Situation, Produce, and the General Disposition of Its Inhabitants: An Inquiry into the Rise and Progress of the Slave Trade, Its Nature and Lamentable Effects*. 1st publ. Philadelphia, 1771 and London, 1772. *The Project Gutenberg*. 18.Aug.2006 <http://www.gutenberg.org/files/11489/11489-h/11489-h.htm#X >.

Clarkson, Thomas. *An Essay on the Slavery and Commerce of the Human Species, Particularly the African, Translated from a Latin Dissertation, which was Honoured with the First Prize in the University of Cambridge, for the Year 1785, With Additions*. 1786. Whitefish: Kessinger Publishing , no year.

---. *An Essay on the Impolicy of the African Slave Trade: In Two Parts*. 1788. Freeport and New York: Books for Libraries Press, 1971.

---. "Thoughts on the Necessity of Improving the Condition of the Slaves in the British Colonies, With a View to their Ultimate Emancipation; and on the Practicability, the Safety, and the Advantages of the Latter Measure." London, 1823. *Slavery, Abolition, and Emancipation: Writings in the British Romantic Period. Vol. 3. The Emancipation Debate*. Ed. Debbie Lee. London: Pickering and Chatto, 1999. 85-144.

---. *The History of the Rise, Progress and Accomplishment of the Abolition of the African Slave Trade by the British Parliament*. 1839. Whitefish: Kessinger Publishing, no year.

Hobbes, Thomas. Introduction. *Leviathan*. 1651. 12.11.2006 <http://www.gutenberg.org/dirs/etext02/lvthn10.txt>.

Smith, Adam. "An Inquiry into the Nature and Causes of the Wealth of Nations." 11th ed, 2002. *The Project Gutenberg*: 5.Sept.2006 <http://www.gutenberg.org/dirs/etext02/wltnt11.txt>.

Locke, John. "Two Treatises of Government: Of Civil-Government – Book II." 1st publ. 1690. *The Project Gutenberg*. 16. Aug.2006 <http://www.gutenberg.org/dirs/etext05/trgov10h.htm>.

Wheatley, Phillis. “On Being Brought from Africa to America.” 2.Nov.2006. <http://www.vcu.edu/engweb/webtexts/Wheatley/brought.html >.

*The New Testament and Psalms: New International Version.* Lutherworth: The Gideons International, no year.

The *History*, the *Essay*, and *Thoughts* are also available online: <http://www.gutenberg.org/browse/authors/c#a3503>

Criticism:

Althusser, Louis. “Ideology and Ideological State Apparatuses.” *Lenin and Philosophy and Other Essays.* London: New Left Books, 1971. 124-173.

Anstey, Roger. *The Atlantic Slave Trade and British Abolition : 1760-1810.* Aldershot : Gregg Revivals, 1992.

---, ed. *Liverpool, the African Slave Trade, and Abolition : Essays to Illustrate Current Knowledge and Research.* Liverpool: Historic Society of Lancashire and Cheshire, 1976.

Ashworth, John. “The Relationship between Capitalism and Humanitarianism.” *The Antislavery Debate: Capitalism and Abolitionism as a Problem in Historical Interpretation.* Ed. Thomas Bender. Berkeley, Los Angeles and London: University of California Press, 1992. 180-199.

Barker, Chris: *Cultural Studies: Theory and Practice.* 2nd ed. London, Thousand Oaks, New Delhi: Sage Publications, 2004.

Bender, Thomas. Introduction. *The Antislavery Debate: Capitalism and Abolitionism as a Problem in Historical Interpretation.* Ed. Thomas Bender. Berkeley, Los Angeles and London: University of California Press, 1992. 1-13.

Bulmer, Martin, and John Solomos. Introduction. *Racism.* Eds. Martin Bulmer and John Solomos. Oxford: University Press, 1999. 3-17.

Carey, Brycchan. *British Abolitionism and the Rhetoric of Sensibility: Writing, Sentiment and Slavery, 1760-1807.* Houndsmill and New York: Palgrave Macmillan, 2005.

Curtin, Philip. “The Africans’ ‘Place in Nature.’” *Racism.* Eds. Martin Bulmer and John Solomos. Oxford: University Press, 1999. 31-34.

Craton, Michael, James Walvin, and James Wright, eds. *Slavery, Abolition and Emancipation: Black Slaves and the British Empire: A Thematic Documentary*. London: Longman, 1976.

Davis, David Brion. "Abolitionism and Ideological Hegemony." *The Antislavery Debate: Capitalism and Abolitionism as a Problem in Historical Interpretation*. Ed. Thomas Bender. Berkeley, Los Angeles, and London: University of California Press, 1992. 161-179.

---. *Slavery and Human Progress*. New York and Oxford: Oxford University Press, 1986.

---. "Slavery and 'Progress.'" *Antislavery, Religion, and Reform: Essays in Memory of Roger Anstey*. Eds. Christine Bolt, and Seymour Drescher. Folkestone, Kent: Dawson Archon, 1980. 335-366.

---. "The Problem of Slavery in the Age of Revolution, 1770-1823." *The Antislavery Debate: Capitalism and Abolitionism as a Problem in Historical Interpretation*. Ed. Thomas Bender. Berkeley, Los Angeles and London: University of California Press, 1992. 27-103.

---. *The Problem of Slavery in the Age of Revolution, 1770-1823*. Ithaca: Cornell University Press, 1975.

Drescher, Seymour. *Capitalism and Antislavery: British Mobilization in Comparative Perspective*. New York and Oxford: Oxford University Press, 1987.

---. *Econocide: British Slavery in the Era of Abolition*. Pittsburgh: Universtity of Pittsburgh Press, 1977.

---. *The Mighty Experiment: Free Labor Versus Slavery in British Emancipation*. Oxford: Oxford University Press, 2002.

Eltis, David, ed. *The Abolition of the Atlantic Slave Trade: Origins and Effects in Europe, Africa, and the Americas*. Madison: University of Wisconsin Press, 1981.

Fairclough, Norman. *Language and Power*. 2nd ed. Harlow: Pearson Education Limited, 2001.

Gibson Willson, Ellen. *Thomas Clarkson: A Biography*. York: William Sessions Limited, 1989.

Gramsci, Antonio. *Selections from the Prison Notebook.* Eds. Quintin Hoare, and Geoffrey Nowell Smith. New York: International Publishers, 1971.

Haskell, Thomas L. "Capitalism and the Origins of Humanitarian Sensiblity, Part 1." *The Antislavery Debate: Capitalism and Abolitionism as a Problem in Historical Interpretation.* Ed. Thomas Bender. Berkeley, Los Angeles and London: University of California Press, 1992. 107-135.

---. "Capitalism and the Origins of Humanitarian Sensiblity , Part 2." *The Antislavery Debate: Capitalism and Abolitionism as a Problem in Historical Interpretation.* Ed. Thomas Bender. Berkeley, Los Angeles and London: University of California Press, 1992. 136-160.

Hawker, Sara, Catharine Soanes, and Alan Spooner, eds. *Oxford Paperback Dictionary, Thesaurus, and Wordpower Guide.* Oxford: Oxford University Press, 2001.

Hochschild, Adam. *Bury the Chains: The British Struggle to Abolish Slavery.* London: Pan Books, 2006.

Jennings, Judith. *The Business of Abolishing the British Slave Trade: 1783 – 1807.* London: Cass, 1997.

Jordan, Michael. *The Great Abolition Sham: The True Story of the End of the British Slave Trade.* Stroud: Sutton Publ., 2005.

Kitson, Peter. "'Candid Reflections': The Idea of Race in the Debate over the Slave Trade and Slavery in the Late Eighteenth and Early Nineteenth Century." *Discourses of Slavery and Abolition: Britain and its Colonies, 1760-1838.* Eds. Brycchan Carey, Markman Ellis, and Sara Salih. Houndsmill and New York: Palgrave Macmillan, 2004. 11-25.

Lee, Debbie. *Slavery and the Romantic Imagination.* Philadelphia: Univ. of Pennsylvania Press, 2004.

Mosse, George. "Eighteenth-Century Foundations." *Racism.* Eds. Martin Bulmer and John Solomos. Oxford: University Press, 1999. 40-44.

Oldfield, John R. *Popular Politics and British Ant-Slavery: The Mobilisation of Public Opinion against the Slave Trade, 1787-1807.* London: Frank Cass Publishers, 1998.

Said, Edward W. *Orientalism.* New York: Vintage Books, 1979.

Shakespeare, William. *The Complete Works of William Shakespeare.* London: Oxford University Press, 1957.

Temperley, Howard. "Antislavery as a Form of Cultural Imperialsm." *Antislavery, Religion, and Reform: Essays in Memory of Roger Anstey.* Eds. Christine Bolt and Seymour Drescher. Hamden: Dawson, 1980. 335-350.

Trevelyan, George M. *Geschichte Englands.* Vol. 2. München and Berlin: Oldenbourg, 1936.

Turley, David. *The Culture of English Antislavery: 1780-1860.* London: Routledge, 1991.

Van Dijk, Teun A. "Multidisciplinary CDA: A Plea for Diversity." *Methods of Critical Discourse Analysis.* Eds. Ruth Wodak, and Michael Meyer. London: Sage Publications 2001. 95-120.

---. "Critical Discourse Analysis." *The Handbook of Discourse Analysis.* Eds. Deborah Schiffrin, Deborah Tannen, and Heidi E. Hamilton. Oxford: Blackwell, 2001. 352-371.

Walvin, James, ed. *Slavery and British society: 1776 – 1846.* Baton Rouge: Louisiana State University Press, 1982.

Wheeler, Roxann. *The Complexion of Race: Categories of Difference in Eighteenth-Century British Culture.* Pennsylvania: University of Pennsylvania Press, 2000.

Online sources:

Carey, Brycchan. *Biography of Thomas Clarkson.* 8. Aug. 2006 <http://www.brycchancarey.com/abolition/clarkson.html>.

Kershaw, Simon. "The Good & The Great: Thomas Clarkson." *Diocese of Ely.* 8.Aug. 2006 <http://ely.anglican.org/about/good_and_great/tclarkson.html>.

"Thomas Clarkson." *The Antislavery Society*. 22. Aug. 2006 <http://www.antislaverysociety.org/>.

***ibidem*-Verlag**
Melchiorstr. 15
D-70439 Stuttgart

info@ibidem-verlag.de

www.ibidem-verlag.de
www.edition-noema.de
www.autorenbetreuung.de

Zeitfracht Medien GmbH
Ferdinand-Jühlke-Straße 7
99095 Erfurt, Deutschland
produktsicherheit@kolibri360.de